Praise for

"Grant Menzies has done it a̲ bright and dazzling life back into a most magnificent little dog who last padded the earth a century ago. (And in a bizarre twist, 'came to life' again during the Second World War.) Through his phenomenal research, and his beautiful prose, Menzies resurrects not only the beloved four-legged central character, but the whole era around the Great War. A fascinating read about the world during a devastatingly difficult time, and the dog who helped so many get through it. Enjoy it with a cup of tea by the hearth with your best friend at your side."

—Maria Goodavage, author of *Doctor Dogs: How Our Best Friends Are Becoming Our Best Medicine* and *Secret Service Dogs: The Heroes Who Protect the President of the United States*

"This book is about Muggins, a small white dog who played an inspiring role supporting the war effort during WWI. However it is more than that. It is a snapshot of the people and the times on the home front. It also provides heartwarming insights into the nature of the human–canine bond. It is an example of fascinating historical detective work and great writing. A must-read for dog lovers and history buffs."

—Stanley Coren, author of *The Intelligence of Dogs: A Guide to the Thoughts, Emotions, and Inner Lives of Our Canine Companions*

"A fascinating account of the life of an important dog, Muggins—who worked the docks and streets of Victoria to raise funds for charity—and a poignant and thoughtful reflection on the role of dogs in wartime."

—Zazie Todd, PhD, author of *Wag: The Science of Making Your Dog Happy*

Praise for *Muggins*

"*Muggins* is not only a colourful and touching love letter to the little white Spitz of Victoria but to all dogs who selflessly devote themselves to us humans, in wartime and in peace times. May we always rise to display the fine qualities our dogs believe us to have."

—Susan Raby-Dunne, military historian, battlefield guide, and author of *Bonfire: The Chestnut Gentleman*

"Grant Hayter-Menzies has spun a true and eminently readable tale about a dog, about a city, and about a war. Through the author's journey of discovery in search of a little Spitz legend, and his own personal stories, Muggins is brought to life in a way no taxidermist could ever do. The true stories of animals whose training and loyalty earned them a supporting and sometimes deadly role in the terrors of war give us unique portals into history. Hayter-Menzies weaves an endearing account of the impact and appeal of a canine in the limelight, whose dogged loyalty throughout his short life made him a bona fide hero of the war effort on the home front. This almost irresistible account belongs on a unique shelf of tales of animal heroes of the Great War, with Michael Morpurgo's *War Horse* and *Winnie's Great War* by Lindsey Mattuck and Josh Greenhut, the story of Winnipeg, the bear who inspired A.A. Milne's Pooh Bear."

—Jacqueline Carmichael, author of *Heard Amid the Guns: True Stories from the Western Front 1914-1918*

MUGGINS

MUGGINS

*The Life and Afterlife of a
Canadian Canine War Hero*

GRANT HAYTER-MENZIES

FOREWORD BY MARK ZUEHLKE

HERITAGE

Heritage House Publishing Company Ltd.
heritagehouse.ca

Cataloguing information available from Library and Archives Canada
978-1-77203-371-7 (paperback)
978-1-77203-372-4 (ebook)

Edited by Renée Layberry
Proofread by Nandini Thaker
Cover design by Jacqui Thomas
Interior book design by Colin Parks
Cover photographs: Drawing of Muggins (top) courtesy of
    Christine O'Brien, and Image J-01499 courtesy of the
    Royal BC Museum and Archives

The interior of this book was produced on 100% post-consumer
paper, processed chlorine free and printed with vegetable-based inks.

Heritage House gratefully acknowledges that the land on which we
live and work is within the traditional territories of the Lkwungen
(Esquimalt and Songhees), Malahat, Pacheedaht, Scia'new, T'Sou-ke,
and W̱SÁNEĆ (Pauquachin, Tsartlip, Tsawout, Tseycum) Peoples.

We acknowledge the financial support of the Government of Canada
through the Canada Book Fund (CBF) and the Canada Council for
the Arts, and the Province of British Columbia through the British
Columbia Arts Council and the Book Publishing Tax Credit.

25 24 23 22 21   1 2 3 4 5

Printed in Canada

To die a dog's death once was held for shame.
Not all men so beloved and mourned shall lie
As many of these, whose time untimely came
To die.

His years were full: his years were joyous: why
Must love be sorrow, when his gracious name
Recalls his lovely life of limb and eye?

If aught of blameless life on earth may claim
Life higher than death, though death's dark wave rise high,
Such a life as this among us never came
To die.

—A.C. SWINBURNE (1837–1909),
"At a Dog's Grave"

He is very imprudent, a dog is. He never makes it
his business to inquire whether you are in the right
or in the wrong, never bothers as to whether you are
going up or down upon life's ladder, never asks whether
you are rich or poor, silly or wise, sinner or saint.
You are his pal. That is enough for him.

—JEROME K. JEROME,
Idle Thoughts of an Idle Fellow

FOR RUDI AND FREDDIE

IN MEMORY OF BILL

AND OF DAD

AND GRANDPA

WITH LOVE

CONTENTS

FOREWORD

I AM LOOKING AT A GRAINY BLACK-AND-WHITE photograph taken on October 19, 1919, on the steps leading to the entrance of Victoria's Empress Hotel. Pictured are—if I may be so bold—two of Canada's most famous Great War personages. One is General Sir Arthur Currie. He's in full uniform with one almost knee-high boot, complete with spurs, on one step and the other on the step below. While looking directly at the camera, his body is turned to one side. This is because he is facing a small, white Spitz-breed dog who is sitting with his front paws up; his face is also directed to the camera. You can imagine which of the subjects is the more adorable.

The dog is Muggins, the Red Cross dog who, by 1919, had become an international celebrity. The photograph held by the Saanich Archives is credited to Beatrice Woodward, who owned Muggins. When war broke out, Muggins was volunteered by Beatrice to fundraise for the Canadian Red Cross, wandering the streets of Victoria with little tin boxes strapped to his side that people could put money into. He ultimately raised about $21,000, which today would likely be equivalent to a quarter million dollars. For his efforts, Muggins would be awarded eight medals. According to an undated list signed off by Mrs. Henry Baker (sister of Beatrice Woodward), the medals consisted of: a Red Cross medallion with clasp; a medal from the Croix Rouge Française; a gilded badge "Auxiliary" FOO (Forward Observation Officer); a YMCA emblem; medallion from the Esquimalt Military Hospital; a medallion presented by the GWVA (Great War Veterans' Association) branch in Victoria, BC; a bar pin with enamel American flag; and a medal with bar from HMS *Lancaster*, dated May 31, 1916.

The pin giving Muggins the honourary rank of FOO—an observing officer acting on behalf of the battery commander—has never been found, and in a full-page article about Muggins in the October 22, 1939, *Daily Colonist*, a photograph shows only seven medals. It's interesting to note that this is precisely the same number of the eight honours General Currie, first commander of the Canadian Corps from 1917 to 1919, received while leading the nation's troops to victory. Given the international attention showered on Muggins, the diminutive dog probably outdistanced Currie (who had his enemies even after his triumphs) in the fame department.

Within a year of meeting Currie, Muggins died. But his fame—and, for some time, his taxidermied remains—carried on. While the remains eventually disappeared, his renown persisted. The story behind how Muggins became an international star is the subject of the book that you are now reading. While focusing on Muggins, his unique life, and unusual contribution

to the nation's war effort, this tender story is also a
reflection on the human–canine relationship, not only
in times of war, but in general. It is also the story of a
city, Victoria, which during the Great War was a bastion
of the British Empire outside of the United Kingdom.
Muggins became a symbol of the empire, and so this
is not only his story but a study of the relationship
between the city and the empire. For many Canadians,
like Currie, the war sowed the seeds of nationalism,
eventually placing Canada at the centre of their hearts
and displacing loyalty to empire. Was Muggins one of
the last symbols of the empire or a symbol of that new
national pride fostered by the suffering Canada experienced in war and its role in the ultimate victory? That's
a question to ponder while reading this entertaining
and informative account.

—MARK ZUEHLKE

PROLOGUE

IMAGINE AN AERIAL VIEW FROM ONE OF THE biplanes sent aloft in the years after the Great War. The sight is not of the scarred battlefields of Great War Europe but of Victoria, British Columbia, the last outpost of the British Empire. The provincial capital would have appeared to have gathered its entire population on the sprawling lawns of the seaside capital's handsome granite Parliament Buildings.

It was the last full week of September 1919. The war to end all wars had been declared at an end almost a year earlier, though the act of doing so had not vanquished the urge nor the incentives to remake another global conflict two decades later.

Yet the apparent dying down of the mayhem which had torn whole nations into pieces gave way to a season when that same world, hoping to heal, had a chance to catch its breath, to give thanks for life and shed tears for the dead. Amid this comparative calm and the sea of Victorians gathered in front of the legislature that early autumn day, the short, boyishly good-looking, slightly nervous, and more than slightly bored heir to the British throne, Edward, Prince of Wales, wearing military uniform, sauntered down a path from the garlanded arched entrance of the Parliament Buildings, the pavement under his boots scattered with flowers tossed by children dressed in angelic white on either side. He came to a stop at a dais built around a polished granite plinth fixed at the bottom of the lawn. There, the prince squinted in the light and turned to smile in response to cheers from the crowd.

This—being put on public display like a purebred dog at a bench show—was what Edward, who would much rather have been at the ranch he'd just bought in Alberta, acidly referred to in a letteras "princing."

By way of an explanation for his presence (for Victoria was but one stop of many on a whirlwind tour of Canada that had begun only a month earlier), an inscription chiselled into the granite behind him in sturdy square capitals proclaimed THIS STONE WAS LAID SEPTEMBER 24, 1919 BY HIS ROYAL HIGHNESS THE PRINCE OF WALES.

Past Edward's left shoulder loomed the high mansard rooflines of the Empress Hotel, named for his great-grandmother Queen Victoria, Empress of India. The empress herself, in bronze, was to rise again, on the plinth behind the prince, in a statue that still peers humourlessly across the sheet of silvery Inner Harbour water. She would be depicted taller and more glamorous than in homely reality, much the way this prince had become a media star and even a sex symbol (as such was understood in 1919) despite a fatally flawed character and a slight physical presence,which was to earn him the moniker, courtesy of Wallis Simpson, the woman he loved, of "the little man." Holding a special silver trowel while the heavy stone was set in place, the Prince of Wales then handed the tool to an attaché, who passed it along to a government employee, who saw to it that the instrument was sent to the archives for preservation.

It may have been at that moment that Edward turned to address a dog, who sat at his feet looking up at him.

A Spitz—the large variety of Pomeranian favoured by Queen Victoria, to such degree that she allowed one of them to stand on her tea table and another one to keep her company on her deathbed—measuring about a foot high at the shoulders, with a pure white coat that made him visible even among crowds of soldiers sailing him around the harbour, and tender brown eyes described as "speaking," the dog waiting on the heir's commentary was called Muggins.

Muggins lived in the home of a patriotic Canadian woman of English origin called Beatrice Woodward. By the time he was about seven years old, Muggins had spent most of his life in Victoria raising the modern equivalent of a quarter of a million dollars, much of it for the Red Cross but also for wounded soldiers at home, for food packets sent to Canadian prisoners of war, for orphaned children and animals injured in war, for relief programs aiding Jews whose homes and livelihoods were destroyed through the devastating effects of ever-shifting front-line battle, and for the starving peoples of Belgium and Italy. Among the hundreds of letters Muggins received from grateful military and civilian admirers alike, one came from a soldier who claimed he would have died if it were not for the food items Muggins's fundraising efforts had sent to him in his German prison.

For his meeting with Prince Edward, Muggins wore his own customary uniform, consisting of a leather harness to which were attached (under lock and key) two rectangular Fry's cocoa tins. These were sometimes covered in the Red Cross logo or those of other charities for which he was collecting, sometimes left to advertise their former contents. (Today, his tins were marked with the acronym GWVA, the Great War Veterans' Association, a group for which the dog raised funds post-war.) Beatrice Woodward would command Muggins to stand still while she fitted the contraption over his head and body. Slots in the lids permitted donors to drop in coins and bills, and these they often did, the tourists visiting the city on the ships that constantly sailed across the Pacific or from across the Strait of Juan de Fuca, to such generous effect that Muggins struggled to carry his clinking saddlebags back up Government Street to the Red Cross HQ on Fort Street several blocks away. On at least one occasion, a concerned citizen, observing the little dog slowly and unsteadily climbing the thirteen stone steps to headquarters offices above, had alerted the police to a possible case of animal cruelty, only to watch Muggins, freed of his burden of benevolence, rush back downstairs with his empty tins and trot out into the street to do it all over again.

No doubt the tins were empty for today's event, or at least for the photo opportunity with the prince. Captured by a camera's lens, Muggins stands looking as nervous as Edward, though like the heir this was hardly his first time as centre of attention or as recipient of the applause of countless strangers.

A young girl wearing white lace and ribbons—Doris Baker, niece of Beatrice Woodward—stepped forward, curtsied to the prince, and made a short speech about the wonder dog at their feet. She finished by offering the prince a photograph of Muggins. With the premier of British Columbia, the Hon. John Oliver, on one side, and Sir Francis Stillman Barnard, Provincial Lieutenant Governor, on the other, the prince accepted the photograph from Miss Baker, saying, "You love Muggins, I love Muggins, Victoria and the whole Empire love Muggins. I shall treasure this picture of this grand dog and keep it among my souvenirs at home in London."

Then, to Muggins, Edward said:

> Among the defenders of civilization may be reckoned some of the four-footed creatures. Thanks, Muggins, thanks again and again, for to you as well as other animal friends of man is due a large portion of the Empire's success. Muggins, in the name of the Empire, I salute you.[1]

More applause—and the sturdy little Muggins may have offered his trademark salute, sitting back on his haunches, lifting up his sharp nose to the sky and waving his front paws. We know he licked the prince's friendly hand.

At that point, the prince and his entourage walked back up the flower-strewn pathway, and Muggins was led away, his photograph secured among the prince's papers by an adjutant, and the "grand dog's" brush with human grandeur was over. But not Muggins's fame. This would continue for some time, at least, even after his tragic death, which occurred only a little over three months from his day in the sun with the

Prince of Wales. And with the macabre sentimentality of a hunting trophy expertly rendered by a taxidermist to stare down from a wall or from the dim recesses of a glass case, Muggins would "live" on, raising more funds during another world war, one in which more animals, innocent of causing it, would pay the highest of prices to win it. Four-footed defenders of civilization indeed.

Only a few years after that conflict was concluded, all that remained of Muggins by then—a length of the white fur, removed from his deteriorating body preserved almost thirty years before—was rolled up on a shelf in a house in Victoria. Ultimately, this was to disappear entirely also, leaving us only photographic evidence, in static postcard images and grainy newsreel film, and sheaves of newspaper articles, and vague human memory, that he ever existed.

"Trying to understand a dog's perspective," writes Alexandra Horowitz, "is like being an anthropologist in a foreign land."[2]

Even a dog as heavily covered by the media of his time, and featured in the recorded memories of those who met him and in the many photographs of him in action, largely remains terra incognita. We can scarcely claim that he did what he did for the reasons we would like to think he did them, as if any animal integrated into purely human situations is aware that they are helping win a war or bring happiness to elderly dementia patients by reminding them of earlier times.

As Dale Peterson notes, the way we humans are wired makes us virtually incapable "of accepting an alternative value system as entirely valid—and so, in looking for animal morality, we make the first mistake, which is to search for a system of values that perfectly reflects our own."[3] And what we know of Muggins's story, like that of all animals conscripted to human uses and agendas, is sad, sweet, conflicted, and complex. It is the story of a dog taught to carry out tasks in a time of worldwide conflict, in succour of human suffering brought on by purely human miscalculation, political misjudgement, and a catastrophic failure to value peace over bloodshed. As such, though he was on the comparatively protected receiving end—hospitals—of what a battlefield could do to soldiers, rather than serving among them on the field of battle, Muggins's work in the quiet backwater of Victoria was no different to the more dramatic fates of the pet dogs donated by English families to run messages through tangles of barbed wire and the remains of unlucky dead, a piece of paper tucked into the collar that, if delivered, could save numberless human lives.

Too often, a dispatch dog's life was the price it paid for preserving those human fighters. These dogs—like the human foot soldiers delivered to enemy guns, where, in poet John Mansfield's words, each of their "blind soul[s] is flung upon the air"—were just doing what they were told. They were also clearly doing what they did because they had a manifest desire to serve that outweighed all personal considerations.

Muggins must be seen in this context because what he did—whether he fully understood it, whether he always wanted to do it—made a difference in some ways that are obvious and quantifiable and in others mysterious and incalculable. The joy this dog brought to wounded veterans convalescing in hospital, or to troops departing—with excitement and fear—for the front, or to nurses exhausted and disheartened by bloodshed and pain, is obvious from the photographs and extant newsreel footage, and even more so in the fact that Muggins, despite his short life, has not been forgotten. The fact that an entire family, scattered across the globe, are alive today, descendants of a prisoner of war to whom Muggins's fundraising efforts sent food and comfort packages, is ample testament to one little dog's tireless work.

My writing's focus on the animal–human dynamic did not come out of the blue.

All my conscious life—as guardian of many animal companions since my boyhood, and as student of the history of what humans do to animals and what animals do for us—I've been fascinated and moved by the way we interact with animals and the way they interact with us.

Through my research into the lives of animals conscripted into service in wars no animal ever caused, I have also been heartbroken by this interaction. Without bravery, that desperate self-medication that gets us through death in the family, cancer diagnosis, bitter divorce, none of us would step willingly into disaster, self-imposed or imposed upon us from outside. But as human animals, we have a choice. The skinny lad from Aberdeen who was my grandfather, rushing to be accepted into the brotherhood in hell that was the Great War—even Granddad could have closed the door of his young life to that pit of destruction that swallowed so many. Yet he chose to go in and he somehow survived the consequences of his choice, one which so many did not.

No animal has that opportunity because they live in a world in which we have imposed roles on them—roles around labour for us, around serving as our food, as our entertainment, as subjects for painful and often pointless lab tests for human medicine (when one considers that we are in an era of computer models with advanced algorithms, which can more efficiently and accurately replace living test subjects).

What makes the role of animals in war especially terrible is that no animal ever started a battle. No animal could conceive of a conflict between nations, creeds, or parties that spirals into armed violence, pitting whole populations against each other for gain at any price, for such is any conflict that accepts that the sacrifice of human life is a proper bargain in order to win. Animals know nothing of contested boundaries or of specious treaties behind the gleaming ribbons of which lurk the poisons of war when agreement breaks down—as it seems to do all too frequently in the course of human history.

We should not—we must not—call them heroes, not as heroes embody heroism. Humans rush in, to paraphrase an old saw, where saner souls jump clear. Humans understand the rules, accept justifications for risking their lives for an idea or ideal. Leave that heroism to humankind.

It has been and always will be argued whether an animal is capable of understanding what it has been called on and coerced to do. For all the tests by scientists, all the studies and observations conducted by behavioural experts, we will likely never know. All we have to really go by is the animal's response, and this is hotly debated. Horses and mules put to the violent uses of war might shy or balk, or gallop straight into battle, depending on circumstances and the nature of the individual animal. A dog might sit and shiver under gunfire, though "trained" to endure it, while another, comparatively unexposed, might dash into a hail of shrapnel at human command in an especially tragic example of the old trope of a dog living (or, in this case, dying) to please its master. This is a tragic dynamic of power and powerlessness, which we have exploited, often unwittingly, even more often cruelly, to achieve purely human goals, since the advent of recorded time.

Given all this, what is the significance of Muggins's brief life, which was never threatened in service to actual warfare? Muggins spent the majority of his seven years in Victoria, a languid city even in wartime, a place of flowers and afternoon tea and retired English civil servants from India who preserved imperial Englishness as a virtue long after it ceased to colour the map of half the world a particular pink. Muggins did not hear massed guns except those on his first and last Remembrance Day in November 1919. He saw only the soldiers whose lives war had spared if not their legs, hands, eyes, or sanity; the only generals he met were exhausted, somewhat puzzled, and brooding men who posed with him, their medals glittering in the sunlight denied to so many of the vanished men they had led into battle.

Yet Muggins's efforts—and those of the several other Victoria dogs conscripted with him to aid the war effort and to raise funds for post-war causes—are fascinating in their own right, as a glimpse of the type of benevolent creativity developed and harnessed for action on the home front. This concerted campaign to mop up and process war's terrible aftermath was almost exclusively spearheaded by women—Muggins's human, Beatrice Woodward, was a prime example of this type of "home front" woman and of the high degree of energy and courage they displayed setting to rights a world tipped roughly on its side by warring men. They and Muggins shared something important in common—a need arose, and they were quick to meet it.

Muggins's life and how he spent it raises all the critical points of animal welfare discussed above—the role of animals in human warfare, in which sentimentality and exploitation face off over an innocent animal, which, of course, has no choice about the matter. Muggins was clearly devoted to the soldiers he visited in hospital, to the nurses he followed on their rounds, to the women who used him to raise funds for other women's sons, brothers, and husbands who had survived the war, as theirs had not, and perhaps simply to that abstract sense of being useful that every dog, from sheep herders to aristocrats like Muggins, seems born with and must act upon when called—and even when not.

Muggins's life, their lives, matter, whatever humans may do to obfuscate their intelligence or sentimentalize their motivations.

For this reason alone, the story of the famous Red Cross dog of Victoria, who helped the wounded endure, the starving eat, and the dispirited have hope again, demands to be told—not as the dusty, sadly immobile, and lifeless corpse set up for public display by a taxidermist, but as the living, breathing, feeling little dog whose memory has never left the streets of the city where he worked nor the hearts of those who remember and value courage and devotion.

Above all, Muggins—like all the dogs we love—was able to galvanize the better selves of the humans around him in a way that old-fashioned guilt can never do. All who have lived with a dog know this. Because of our dogs, our moral compass finds itself pointing to true north; to be lesser people than they think we are seems an unbearable failing to any human with a conscience. My dog Freddie makes me want to be as good as he believes me to be. So for him, I try my best, as Muggins inspired all about him to do during his lifetime and in the long afterlife guaranteed by fame.

CHAPTER 1

A Dog's Life

I FIRST HEARD OF MUGGINS, THE FAMOUS—AND, TO me, then, utterly unknown—fundraising dog of Great War Victoria, on Remembrance Day in 2015, close to ninety-five years after his death.

The setting was Tanner's Books in Sidney, a community north of Victoria on the Saanich Peninsula, then my hometown with my then-partner and our rescue dog, a Spitz called Freddie, who is still very much part of my life.

That day, I was signing copies of my newly released biography of Rags (1916–1936), the Paris stray who became mascot to the American First Division in 1918, saving hundreds of lives running messages through cratered battlefields, as well as saving the spirits and sanity of soldiers who, but for Rags, did not have a whole lot to look forward to from day to day in the depths of warfare and bloodshed.

I did more than sit there signing books.

People had approached me that afternoon with emotion in their faces, having been touched by the book's cover, showing Rags with one of the soldiers who'd rescued him off the streets of Paris in July 1918, or who were moved by the day's memories to explore further. One woman was different. Wearing all black, she came up with a smile, looked at my book, with its cover photo, put it down, and began to weep. I hurried around the table to comfort her. She told me through tears that her son was in the Canadian Forces and had had to leave his beloved dog behind in Alberta; his subsequent efforts to get postings as near to home, and the dog, had failed. She wanted to buy a copy of my book for her son, to help him get through his posting. I wrote something special in the book for her son, and she talked about happy times he had had with the dog. Off she went, holding the book close under her arm, as if it were a puppy in need of protection from an unfriendly world.

That's when I saw Dr. Sylvia Van Kirk.

Now a retired University of Toronto professor, in 1980 Sylvia published *Many Tender Ties: Women in Fur-Trade Society, 1670–1870*, an important work tracing inter-dependencies between not just colonial trappers and Indigenous Peoples in Canada, but the ties of relation-ships between Indigenous women and those men. It was as if I should be walking up to *her* book signing table, not the other way around, and I rose to greet her.

We chatted about my book, a copy of which she asked me to sign. While I wrote on the flyleaf, Sylvia asked, "Have you ever heard of Muggins?" By that Remembrance Day afternoon in 2015, I had lived and worked in Greater Victoria for almost ten years, but no, I had not heard of Muggins (one of the reasons why I wrote this book). Who or what was Muggins?

Grant Hayter-Menzies

Sylvia chuckled, somewhat grimly; obviously she had faced this response before. Muggins, she told me (as quickly as possible, as a line had begun to form behind her) was a Spitz dog who lived in Victoria. He was snow white in colour and had raised thousands of dollars between 1916 and his death in early 1920 for wartime charities, notably the Red Cross, of which he was an unofficial, much-beloved mascot—pretty much like Rags to the First Division. I knew something of the Red Cross, mainly through studying the life of one of my childhood heroes, Florence Nightingale, who endorsed the founding of the British Red Cross in 1870. I also knew that Nightingale encouraged the presence of animals in the rooms or on the beds of patients dealing with or recovering from illness. "A small animal," she wrote, "is often an excellent companion for the sick," noting that an invalid, asked whether he preferred his nurse or his dog, was apt to point to the latter as the best company in the sick room. I could see, before I knew much else about him, how Muggins could have fulfilled that healing role for which Nightingale believed dogs, especially, so suited.[1]

"I've been collecting material on Muggins for years," Sylvia finished as she pulled away. "He deserves a book, I think. I'd enjoy working on a project about Muggins with you," she added, thanking me for the inscription as others took her place. Then she was gone.

Before she departed, Sylvia and I had exchanged email addresses, and I'd planned to get in touch with her, though not, I admit, because I much looked forward to being a co-author. I had tried this before, and it had never worked out for either myself or my co-conspirator.

For me, writing is an intensely personal, solo act, motivated by the need to learn as much as I can, and to share what I've learned, on a subject of intense interest to me, which I start out knowing mostly nothing about. I write because I am taken up by an idea that makes me lose sleep at night and dream through my days; that sends me on wild goose chases through stacks of other writers' books, where I may find just one fact for all my chasing; that pushes me to arrange eleventh-hour interviews with historic witnesses to history fading fast into old age, even as death waits at their door; that keeps me poring over photographs and newsreels and newspapers and those crisp artifacts of past dialogue, not quite lost on the air, that are old and precious letters.

This search must happen on my own time and my own terms. A writing partnership felt to me like a kind of rotating acting contract, where some days one was the understudy and other days the lead, with all the complex and confusing gear-shifts that implies. This didn't work for me, and as kindly and witty as Sylvia appeared to be, and as much an honour as it would be to work with her, I could not see the idea working out for either of us. (As I would find, her wide-ranging research would be my constant companion as I began to explore the life of Victoria's most famous dog, so she was with me throughout after all.)

But before any decision could be made one way or the other, and not long after that book signing in Sidney, my life shape-shifted in almost every conceivable way. I was confronted with several upheavals in succession: the death of one parent and a diagnosis of Alzheimer's disease for another, a divorce followed by a house sale and move, a job change, and all the other adjustments and readjustments required by circum-stances largely beyond our control, reminding us how little we are actually moored to everything we think will last forever.

Eventually, as it does, life settled into a new if not quite familiar pattern, the way a river, after ravaging floods, finds a new bed to follow. And I began to think again of Muggins.

Even as I worked on two more books, Muggins kept bobbing up, brought to mind when my own dog Freddie, dark where Muggins was light, came up to my desk to gaze at me with his warm brown eyes, so like Muggins's in the photos Sylvia had shared with me, radiating a keen sense of needing to be of service to whatever I needed, and needing to be cared for, too. What were the words poet Mary Oliver put in the eyes of her dog? "Tell me you love me. Tell me again." I see these words in Freddie's eyes, I saw them in the sepia-toned photos of Muggins, too.[2]

Fast forward to spring 2019. I was living in Victoria again, and Sylvia reappeared at another book launch and signing I was holding at Bolen Books in Hillside Mall.

Sylvia sat in the audience listening to me talk about my new book's topic—Woo, the monkey companion of artist Emily Carr, and the powerful effect animals have on human endeavours, always more crucial than we think or know—and afterward stood in line to get my inscription in her copy. Both of us had been through our different challenges over the course of the past several years, and we were as relieved as pleased to see one another again, still upright and still busy with the business of research and discovery.

As I handed her book back to her, Sylvia said, "After tonight, I know it. There is no question. You are the one to write about Muggins. May I show you the materials I've collected?"

The pieces of this dog's life story, previously hanging in the air about us through all the years' wanderings, came together.

I was ready to tell Sylvia that, yes, I very much wanted to see her Muggins collection.

She came to tea at my house a week or so later.

I helped her in with a number of bags she'd brought in her car. We emptied them of their contents in my living room, a mass of clippings, photographs, documents, and everything else Sylvia and her researchers could find over the course of several years.

We talked about Muggins, about the lectures she had given in Victoria on his life and legacy, on the Red Cross's abiding reverence for him, and how everyone else seemed to have forgotten he had ever existed—which was as much reason to write about him as any other. Another reason was the puzzling fact that wherever I looked, including the pages of Ernest Harold Baynes's important 1925 book, *Animal Heroes of the Great War*, who listed all the wartime fundraising mascots he could find information about, there was no mention of Muggins.

Only a few Canadian books dealing with other aspects of the Great War, and these clippings scattered on my living room carpet, spoke of him at all.

This had also been the case for Rags, the former Paris stray who had become mascot to the American First Division in France. His photograph still hangs in First Division Headquarters, but as far as the public knew, the only canine mascot of the Great War was Sergeant Stubby, another former stray who served as mascot of the American 102nd Infantry Regiment and who for some years has stared out of a glass case at the Smithsonian Institution, his many medals glinting in the half-light. Rags, who was buried with military honours, is represented by fading photos in an album and his collar tag—clearly insufficient to get Hollywood calling.

Muggins, it seemed, could, like Rags, also have used a good public relations firm.

After Sylvia departed and I put the tea cups away, I sat on the floor with Freddie and we looked through the binders, folders, and envelopes.

The part of me that is a cunning opportunist was saying, with an inward cackle of glee, "What a treasure trove! And you didn't even have to do any of the work! You just have to make a narrative about his life, following the path Sylvia has already laid out, and how easy is that!"

Over time, a prolific biographer will tend to lean more and more on the shorthand of trusted technique, on tried-and-true methods, between the structural interstices of which he adds whatever creative musings he thinks necessary to telling the truth of a life using appropriate colour and texture, to make the person—or animal—featured live again in the reader's mind.

Looking back over my writing career, I thought of the years of research required for each of my books; the hours spent in archives and libraries; the sidewalks I'd covered as I raced from place to place to piece a life together from disparate materials, sometimes from a half dozen places around the globe. So these neat binders of carefully labelled sections, these folders with their precise content, these notes on everything, is what it must look like to a reader who only knows the end result of all an author's arduous seeking—indeed, not unlike what a book's reader saw upon buying a non-fiction volume and reading it at leisure, unaware except for the many pages of sources just how many pieces of the puzzle had to be found and then fitted into place to create the picture, the narrative, that is coalescing into a story, a life, in their hands.

Sylvia had told me that, far from being a compre-hensive collection of material on Muggins, there were fundamental pieces of the puzzle still missing.

For instance, where was Muggins born? Was his birthplace, as suggested, to be found in the well-appointed house of a Calgary millionaire? Or, as hinted elsewhere, had he been born in Russia? If he wasn't born here, how did Muggins get to Victoria? And if a rich man's pet he was, how did he so easily (as it appeared) become a hard-working canvasser for public donations to the war effort? And there were other ques-tions that, by rights, should have been easily answered. What had happened to the portrait of him by a noted post-war battlefield artist, who spent three years living in tin huts as she captured what war, death, and life had left behind on the fields of France? And what of the POWs who had received Muggins's food packages through the Red Cross, men who were said to have written him letters thanking him for saving their lives? Had they survived to come home? Had they started families? Were there people living today, like the des-cendants of men whose lives were saved by Rags of the First Division, who little knew they owed their lives to the labours of one little dog?

Grant Hayter-Menzies

And what, Sylvia asked me, but really asked the universe—a question I was myself to direct to plenty of starry skies thereafter—what had become of Muggins's body, mounted and preserved and later brought out to raise funds for the Red Cross during the Second World War? Military mascots from the Victorian period may still be seen, frozen in place in glass boxes that stand in pride of place in regimental mess halls or museums. Where was this dog who had changed so many lives, saved so many lives?

What is this little dog's legacy now, despite the ever-rolling river of historical amnesia which seems to follow every war? How shall we appreciate his life? I looked through the binders and folders and notepads, remembering Sylvia gazing into the distance over her tea cup, as if the answers to all these mysteries lay not farther away but closer to, if we could just make them materialize, if we could just take an animal's devotion seriously.

Thanks to Sylvia's research and her directions, I made my first foray into Muggins's life by visiting the Saanich Archives in Victoria, where many of the last remaining palpable objects from his lifetime, including his collection of medals, are kept today as part of a generous donation made to the archives by their owner, Jean Hughes, grand-niece of Beatrice Woodward, Muggins's guardian. This, I thought, would be the closest thing to meeting the little dog that so many had forgotten ever existed.

For me, as biographer, the most salient part of research is visiting the place where my subject lived or died or was buried, and seeing with my own eyes any tangible possessions they may have left behind: house, books, letters, silverware, etc. There are locations associated with Muggins in Victoria, Vancouver, and elsewhere, including the house where he died. But there are very few things he would have touched, making him feel even more like a frail ghost, one whose soul had long since departed.

After looking through a series of clippings about Muggins in a slim folder and viewing a large portrait of him, found in a shop on Fort Street, the back of which held pencilled clues to Muggins's origins that I would only begin to trace after many months of research, a cardboard box with lid was brought out and opened on the table.

Inside, on a bed of brown cloth, lay seven of his eight known citations. Two Red Cross medals, from the Canadian and the French organizations. A brightly enameled YMCA medal dated November 3, 1919, a mere few months before Muggins died. An elegant but somewhat battered medal and bar, looking as if marked by daily wear, from the crew of the HMS *Lancaster*, dated May 31, 1916. "To the memory of those who fell that day," I read, squinting (the date refers to the Battle of Jutland in the North Sea, the first marine engagement of Allied and German naval forces). And I saw the gold medal, replete with an engraved image of Muggins, bestowed on him by the Esquimalt Military Hospital. This, I knew, Muggins had never worn; it had arrived by post after his death in January 1920.

I remember the first time my grandfather allowed me to see his medals from the Great War; they seemed too heavy for being such slender wafers denoting recognition for service on some of the most horrific battlefields in France. Inscrutable as he was, my grandfather told me little about his experiences in the Great War, and his medals did even less to inform me, making me guess, engaging my imagination, never revealing the hard truths behind the gold, silver, and enamel. (Only one of my grandfather's medals, a handsome bronze disc, makes it clear what victory it marked: a tug-of-war contest behind the lines, in which my grandfather was a member of the winning team.)

I also remember, that first time seeing the medals, how moved I was just to hold them, and decades later, Muggins's awards evoked the same response. Under the watchful eyes of the archivist, I held each medal. I had tears; so did she.

Yet I sensed, after seeing and touching these things from Muggins's life, that there was something intangible I had to find, even more significant than these well-earned medals. What more did I want? What more did I need?

CHAPTER 2

War

WE KNOW THE BASIC OUTLINES OF MUGGINS'S LIFE, though not as much as we know the details of his collection work, these being described at length in newspaper articles during and after the Great War, even up to the present day.

Muggins is assumed to have been born around 1913, as he is described as being seven years old at his death in January 1920.

He first appears in the pages of the *Daily Colonist* in Victoria in 1913 and not again until 1916, when he is already collecting for the Red Cross and other charities. He died on January 14, 1920, of pneumonia, and was mounted by a taxidermist; his stuffed body was brought out during the Second World War to raise funds again for the Red Cross.

The last seen of him was a hank of white hair on a closet shelf in the 1950s, his preserved body having evidently fallen to pieces from exposure to the elements over the years, much as the most elegantly silky fur coat, if not kept from light and heat, begins to stiffen, separate, and crumble.

Despite frequent references to his pedigree (in one instance, he was referred to confidently as "son of two refugee dogs from Russia"; this may be a misreading of his breed description, Siberian Spitz, or some garbling of truth[1]), I was unable to fit him into a specific kennel. In his day and before, there were many Spitzes pictured in the news. Fashionable magazines from before the Great War would have featured photos of various European royals posting with their white Spitz dogs, among them people like Grand Duchess Olga Alexandrovna, sister of Tsar Nicholas II, who sat for portraits with her Spitz. These dogs were referenced as being fixtures in well-to-do Russian households,[2] and this, too, may be responsible for the rumour that Muggins had a Russian origin. Many of these articles would give the kennel name and breeder of the dogs. I could find no such background for Muggins. But by all appearances, Muggins was, as described, a purebred German Spitz, the variety of large Pomeranian, upwards of seventeen pounds, favoured by Queen Victoria and earlier generations of her family, as well as European rulers like King Wilhelm of Württemberg, whose beloved Spitz dogs are depicted along with him in a memorial statue in Stuttgart.

Spitz dogs are thought to have first been brought to England in 1760 by Charlotte of Mecklenburg-Strelitz, consort of King George III, and they were to enjoy popularity at that level of society there and on the Continent; it's a rare portrait, painted or photographic, well into the first decade of the twentieth century, of an aristocrat young or old, that does not include a

Pomeranian dog. Empress Joséphine of France was guardian to a Pomeranian. Composer Wolfgang Amadeus Mozart had a Pomeranian, Pimperl, as did British prime minister William Gladstone, who adored his dog, Petz. And of course, Queen Victoria had several Spitz and Pomeranian dogs in her household.

That is not to say Muggins came of a breed of dog that had been universally loved. As early as 1800, Sydenham Edwards wrote in his *Cynographia Britannica* that "the Pomeranian or Fox-dog" was "of little value as a House Dog, being noisy, artful, and quarrelsome; cowardly, petulant, and deceitful; snappish and dangerous to children; and in other respects without useful properties." One hundred and thirty years later, it would be written of this execrable creature that "every Pomeranian is high-spirited and really gentle and affectionate." Lady Kitty Ritson (1887–1969), who wrote comedies of manners and a book about dogs, and helped introduce the Finnish Spitz to England, wrote after the death of her Pomeranian, "I don't think I can ever keep another [one], for they wind their way round one's heart in a manner that no other member can do."[3]

In Vero Shaw's *The Illustrated Book of the Dog*, published in London in 1881, the author opines that the "Pomeranian is admittedly one of the least interesting dogs in existence," vain of its appearance, less intelligent than it looked, cowardly, deceitful, as if human and dog failings were interchangeable.[4] In "Mad Dog! The Vilification of the White Pomeranian or Spitz Dog in 19th Century New York City," Spitz expert Vivienne Peterson writes of an actual extermination effort mounted in 1870s New York City powered by paranoia that white Spitz dogs—believed of a character "thoroughly and irredeemably corrupt"—were deadly carriers of rabies.[5]

And then we have Queen Victoria who, far from finding the Spitz dog cunning or jealous or cowardly, loved them and depended on them (and on all her dogs of whatever breed) very dearly. After all, this is the queen who had her ginger Spitz, Marco, painted while he was in the process of standing on her tea table, sampling edibles off the Coalport china. It was her white Spitz, Turi, who was filmed in 1896. There he is, standing out purely against the black silk of the queen's perpetual mourning, as Victoria's pony cart is walked around a garden, half the crowned heads of Europe in tow (even as most of them would walk after, not in front of, Caesar, the favourite terrier of King Edward VII, in that king's funeral procession in May 1910, putting Kaiser Wilhelm's precedence-proud nose out of joint). Turi looks perfectly in charge of all the other royals, including Victoria, as well as the staff milling about. Shortly before Victoria died, in January 1901, she asked that Turi be brought up to her bed. He was there when the queen died, a source of comfort to her until the end.[6]

Most dogs of pedigree (unless, like my Freddie, also a purebred Spitz, they were born in a puppy mill) will have in their papers information about where they were born, as well as who their sire and dam were. One of my boyhood dogs, a Saluki I called Rama who was given to me as a gift, had a pedigree that would have shamed many a human royal family. Yet for all his vaunted background, only one source, which offers no further detail, gives Muggins a distinct birthplace. On the back of a framed photographic portrait of the dog donated to

Grant Hayter-Menzies

the Saanich Archives in 2015, the photograph's original owner, after pencilling a note about Muggins's career (the accuracy of which would seem to indicate a close connection to him or to his guardians), added: "He was raised by Mrs. W.R. Hull of Calgary & latterly owned by Mrs. Woodward."[7]

What is clear is that Mrs. Hull of Calgary must be none other than the former Emmeline Banister, wife of prominent rancher and philanthropist William Roper Hull, founder of Hull Services, a charity which still supports thousands of Calgary's most vulnerable children and families.[8]

The Hulls, both English-born, had no children themselves. They lived in a large house, demolished in 1970, at 1202 6th Street SW in Calgary, a residence they called Langmore. The house was built between 1902 and 1905, and was to remain Emmeline's home after William's death in 1924.

With its spreading porches and wide stretches of green lawn in the gardens surrounding it, Langmore was as up to date as domestic luxury could hope to achieve in the still-developing city on the Bow River. Was Langmore Muggins's birthplace? It's certainly possible. White Spitz dogs were rife in the Hull household and among their extended family, if family photographs are anything to judge from.

Along with Emmeline Hull, W.R. Hull, and family members, we see these keen-eyed white dogs among the groupings; one photograph in particular features Emmeline posing beside a Spitz seated on a stool or table, a satin ribbon around its neck. There is another photo in the Hull family archives, taken at Langmore, showing Emmeline's relatives and W.R. Hull with a white Spitz dog that was obviously a beloved family pet. Another oft-published photograph of W.R. Hull shows him seated in front of a sideboard crowded with photos, one of which is a *carte de visite* studio portrait of a young man posing with a white Spitz who sits on a table.

The dog that appears in the photo of Emmeline Hull bears a strong resemblance to Lulu, the Spitz pictured in a September 1913 article in Victoria's *Daily Colonist*. Beatrice Woodward is given as the dog's guardian, and this same article is the first known mention and photo in the press of a Spitz called Muggins, whose guardian is a Mrs. W.J. Roper of Oak Bay. If this is *our* Muggins, how did he and Lulu come to be in Victoria? Mr. and Mrs. Roper's family connections may explain.

Edith Grace Roper, née Marescaux, was born in England to a French family from the Pas de Calais with aristocratic Napoleonic connections and a family château. Her English origins were also upper class: her maternal grandfather was James Todd Ruddell, MP for Honiton and director of the South Australian Company, a group of rich English merchants seeking opportunities in South Australia by aiding colonists in settling there. Edith married prominent British Columbia rancher William James Roper Berry, who later truncated his surname to Roper, in 1900. W.J. Roper was also born in England, in 1839, and came to Canada in 1862. He is most famously associated with the Cherry Creek Ranch near Kamloops, which he purchased in 1877. When his nephews William and John Roper Hull came to Canada in 1873, they worked for their uncle at the ranch, and John remained in the area while William, as we've seen, went to Calgary to found his fortunes.[9]

On his retirement from business and the sale of the Cherry Creek Ranch in 1910, white-bearded and pinstriped W.J. Roper moved to Victoria, where he and Edith lived in Oak Bay in a sprawling white house set among natural rock formations at 1456 Beach Drive. (There is evidence that Roper also owned Mossy Rocks, at 2875 Tudor Avenue, which seems to have been used during Roper's brief year of ownership in 1916 as a hospital for wounded veterans.)[10]

This house, demolished long ago, would have been Muggins's first home in the provincial capital. And if he was really born amid the Edwardian luxuries of the Hulls' Langmore in Calgary—unlike Flush, the spaniel of poet Elizabeth Barrett Browning, fledged in a rough working man's cottage in a rural village in Berkshire, and only brought to the Brownings' elegant Wimpole Street mansion in London later on—there would have been nothing in the Ropers' well-appointed Victoria villa to surprise Muggins, though the sight of the ocean must surely have been of interest to a dog from the prairies. (He's never described as having much to do with seawater, however. For example, my Spitz, Freddie, born in the dry British Columbia interior, will never touch salt water but will gladly wade in a freshwater stream.) Muggins was to see a great deal of the Pacific, and even sail long distances on it, in the near future.

In his seventies when he and his wife relocated to Victoria, and possibly not in the best of health then, W.J. Roper became seriously ill in 1913, and after a long period of suffering, which would not have been improved by the real estate collapse that coincided with the start of the war, he died on August 4, 1916, in Victoria. W.R. Hull and Emmeline Hull were in

Victoria at the end of June 1916, possibly to visit William's dying uncle. (W.R. Hull also had Victoria business connections: in August 1914, just when war broke out, he was granted permission to build a store at Fort and Blanshard Streets.)[11]

The first time we encounter Muggins and Beatrice Woodward is on August 6, 1916, when she brought the Spitz downtown to collect donations for the war effort. How did Muggins change hands? It may be that Edith Roper sold or gave him to Beatrice upon her husband's death or even during his last weeks, when we may presume she had no time or energy to care for the dog properly. Financial pressures may have played a role. Or she was already planning to leave Victoria. We simply do not know.

We can similarly venture only guesses as to what Muggins's life was like before he came to live with the Woodwards. It is easy to see much in Muggins's nature that might come from having been an obedient, quiet pet to an elderly and infirm guardian, much as Queen Victoria's Spitz dogs had done with her up to her death in 1901. Muggins was watchful, attentive, disciplined, and eager to please, all traits one might associate with a dog who spent much of his time indoors or otherwise tethered to an elderly person who did not move about very much and who needed the company of a compliant little dog. Perhaps, given the circumstances, W.J. Roper himself asked that his wife find a proper home for Muggins.

In addition to this circumstantial evidence for how Muggins may have arrived in Victoria, we know that both Emmeline Hull and Beatrice Woodward were members of the Imperial Order Daughters of the Empire (IODE). The IODE was a group founded in 1900 to promote patriotism after the Second Boer War by supporting returned soldiers and caring for the graves of the fallen. Significantly for Muggins's story, in fall 1914, several members of the Gonzales chapter of the IODE (though not Beatrice) were featured with their dogs in a *Daily Colonist* article about their work collecting donations for the war effort, in which appears to be the earliest local example of this type of activity on record. It is also significant that Emmeline Hull hosted meetings of the IODE at her home, Langmore, in Calgary.[12]

Thus, despite their widely disparate backgrounds, Emmeline Hull, Edith Roper, and Beatrice Woodward had certain strong features in common. They were Englishwomen who had come to Canada with their husbands; Emmeline and Beatrice were members of the IODE, so they obviously shared that organization's ideals; and it's not a bad guess that all three women shared an abiding interest in dogs.

For the rest, Beatrice was as different from Emmeline and Edith as if she had come not just from another planet but from an entirely different galaxy. While the elder women were brought up in solid middle- and upper-middle class backgrounds, Beatrice Fear Woodward's origins were rooted firmly in the desperate struggles of Victorian and Edwardian West Midlands working class families. An aristocrat himself, Muggins would prove, like every domestic canine, pedigreed or mutt, that loving a dog offered neutral ground, levelling imaginary social class obstructions almost as easily as two dogs being walked in a park or along a street will meet and greet without recourse to the social register. And Muggins was to prove that even a four-legged aristocrat born in a mansion could walk among humans of all types and stripes and bring them together in a common cause of equal concern to all people everywhere.

Writing of the years before the Great War, Ralph Allen assessed the attractiveness of Canada to people from around the world who were looking for a place to make a fresh start. "The travelers set forth on many impulses and from many places," Allen wrote, "some drawn by fear, some by ambition, some by faith, some by gullibility." The message being sent from Canada was simple and inspiring, if loaded, like most propaganda, with more than its fair share of hyperbole: "Whatever ails you, come to western Canada!"[13]

Like many thousands of immigrants to Canada and to any new country, Harry Woodward would have hoped to start his new life with more promising prospects than he'd had in the country he had left behind, the better to support himself now and his family when they joined him later on.

And as many discover, immigration requires a keen appreciation of the work of a jack of all trades as well as a keen sense of humour in adjusting to its uncertainties and demands. Harry would have found himself doing much the same along these lines as he had done in England. On his 1915 attestation—the document providing his basic contact and personal information as part of joining the Canadian Over-Seas Expeditionary Corps—Harry says his current work is that of fireman,

Grant Hayter-Menzies

which is quite a change from the work he was doing before he left England—that of bath attendant, a low-skill and low-wage job in one of the establishments for public bathing that had been in existence since the 1820s. Harry's brother George had done better for himself since arriving in Victoria: he had a steady job with the city's waterworks, which may have served as an avenue for Harry's last job in Canada before going off to war, with the engineering firm of Sir John Jackson Ltd.

A Conservative politician whose work on the Manchester Ship Canal (1894–1895) led to a knighthood, Jackson's global projects covered a broad range: the dockyard in Simon's Town, South Africa; a railway crossing the Andes; the rebuilding of Singapore Harbour. In 1914, his firm received the contract to build a breakwater in Victoria, part of an effort to work around the natural limitations of Victoria Harbour by creating a place where large ships, like ocean liners (and, soon, troop ships) could dock safely and effectively. Ogden Point, as it was then called (now the Breakwater District at Ogden Point) was the solution to this need, becoming ever more crucial to the nation and the war effort in 1914.[14]

For most of the four years he spent living in Victoria, Harry Woodward worked for Sir John Jackson Ltd.[15] It's likely he lived with his brother and sister-in-law, a common enough arrangement back in their working-class communities in England, and if anything, all the more likely because Beatrice came from and married into a family in which women readily stepped in to shoulder the burdens that poverty and unemployment seemed to lower on households least able to cope with them. Only thirteen when her mother died, Beatrice had taken over household duties to help her father bring up her younger siblings, not relinquishing the role until she married at age twenty-two.[16]

We tend to forget, in our world of centralized and more or less effective social services, that the lives of the Victorian and Edwardian poor (and those of plenty of people today) completely lacked safeguards or safety nets or, indeed, anyone who cared outside of religious organizations, which often imposed requirements on the benefits they doled out that recipients were unable or unwilling to accept. And nobody wanted to end up in the poorhouse where, as many feared and many more knew from experience, one did more than end up, but often simply ended. Harry Woodward had been married in March 1908 to a woman called Phoebe Nicklin, the bride already being pregnant. Phoebe gave birth to a son, who died a few months later. She was soon pregnant again. This time, a daughter called Winifred was born and survived; and by 1912, the couple again had a child, another daughter who was called Constance. They clearly could not afford this on whatever wages Harry was able to bring home; such was the endemic poverty of the Woodwards' community and the paucity of employment opportunities that it was judged cheaper for a family, even a new one which had barely got its start, to live apart rather than together.

By the time she was a year old, baby Winifred was listed in the 1911 Census as living with her grandmother and step-grandfather in Wednesfield, a town within smokestack distance of nearby Wolverhampton. This may have been a consequence of Phoebe's pregnancy with Constance. Harry and Phoebe, meanwhile, were not even living in their own household but rooming with Harry's sister, Florence, and her husband William Cotter. Yet even this cost-cutting cohabitation made little dent in their constant grinding poverty. And this is where Beatrice stepped in, probably motivated by the tragic news of Florence's death at only age twenty-eight. Successful in making a home and life for themselves in Canada, George and Beatrice—who do not seem to have been able to have children of their own—offered to take Florence's next youngest, William, known as Willie, back to Victoria with them, which they did in 1913. (Willie's brother, John, the youngest of Florence's children, was taken in by yet another family member, signalling perhaps that the widower was unable to house and feed any of his children at all.) From this point onward, George and Beatrice would regard Willie, who took their surname as his own, as their son. Thus, when Harry himself came to Canada to break the cycle of poverty as his brother had done, he would have joined Willie as extended family became nuclear family in a pleasant house on Gorge Road West, overlooking the smooth waters that linked the Portage Inlet with Victoria Harbour.

Harry would have lived there up to spring 1916, when he joined the Army Medical Corps, in which he had his basic training in the British Columbia interior before being shipped to France. Once there, he was transferred to the Canadian Mounted Rifles, an infantry unit of the Canadian Expeditionary Force formed in Manitoba in 1914. With wife Phoebe still in England, and his second family in Victoria, Harry joined the ranks of other men with people in various parts of the Commonwealth and Empire worried for their safety and watching the news daily. That news could be slow in coming, drawing out the agony of waiting and prolonging the misery when the news was what had been feared.

In those days before the bloodbath of the Somme, sometime in early June 1916 during the battle of Mount Sorrel near Ypres, Harry was captured and taken prisoner by German forces, along with seven other men. They could be considered lucky: in the Mount Sorrel fighting, almost nine thousand Canadians had been killed or wounded, or had disappeared in the action.

The Woodwards, of course, knew nothing of this until a month and some days later. Like others who were waiting for reports of loved ones at the front, George and Beatrice were going about their daily business, trying to keep to a pattern of normalcy: George at work somewhere in the city, Beatrice looking after the house on Gorge Road. Perhaps, as school was out, Willie was in the stone-walled yard playing with Lulu, her fluffy white figure zigzagging across the grass like dandelion fuzz, Beatrice looking up from time to time from her sewing or gardening. When the newspaper arrived, there would have been the familiar chill, almost normal by now. Haunting the relevant pages of the *Daily Colonist* had become a daily ritual for Victorians as for everyone else. The paper regularly published lists of names, casualties boxed in neatly like graves in a family plot, and nobody hoped to ever see a familiar name inscribed there, private grief open to the entire community to examine. Once the war had progressed beyond mere contretemps to be wrapped up by Christmas, into its second and third years, the casualty lists also grew longer. The Canadian government, in tandem with Canadian Expeditionary

Force Headquarters in London, developed a system for handling casualties that was meant to deflect some of the trauma the news of a dead or missing soldier dropped on households across the nation. Staff, to the tune of hundreds, located in Ottawa were given the sad task of sending out the telegrams, a "delicate duty that followed a strict protocol," writes Edward Butts. "Telegraph companies were instructed not to charge for casualty messages, and they were not to deliver to homes after 9 PM."[17]

Whether through such a telegram, or in the "Canadian Casualties" column in the *Daily Colonist*, lives lost or unaccounted for met Beatrice's eye, and as she followed the column down, past the dead and wounded and missing, she read a name that leapt out and swooped through the door of her home, to remain there until the war's end.

Beatrice was no fainting violet. A small, sturdy woman of packhorse build, neat and tidy and determined, with a decisiveness of movement signalling firm intention behind every act, and with a sweet round face that smiled defiantly back at whatever fate chose to throw at her, she would still have been hit hard by the shock.

The Germans, after all, were regarded even outside the yellow press—so keen to call forth to light of day the monsters from everybody's nightmares—as savages capable of any and every crime. Stories and fantastical images of German soldiers defiling and murdering women, killing the helpless elderly, and catching tossed Belgian babies on the ends of their razor-sharp bayonets were rife. Any family hearing that their son, uncle, father, or brother had been captured by the Germans—despite the facts of the matter, in which German forces were not necessarily any more savage than the forces of any of the other countries ranged against them and the other Central Powers—would not be blamed for fearing the worst. When the British ocean liner *Lusitania* was torpedoed by a German U-boat on May 7, 1915, anti-German rage overtook normally quiet Victoria; a rumour flamed through the town that Germans had celebrated the sinking in German-owned businesses, such as bars and hotels, in downtown. A mob poured through the city, smashing out at any business with a German-sounding name or known to be owned by a German. There was also the usual looting by those looking for something other than frontier justice against the Huns. Food and clothing were upended into the streets and scrambled over greedily. Even the lieutenant governor of the province, Francis S. Barnard, was suspect, given that his wife, Martha Loewen, was the daughter of the German-born owners of Loewen and Erb Brewery.[18]

When war came calling at an individual household, and individual fear or grief loomed larger than life, even the madness of mobs receded into the background. And while Beatrice sat in her Gorge Road bungalow absorbing the news, with young Willie and Lulu looking to her for answers, Muggins was far away—literally not more than across town, but he could have been on another planet, in terms of what they were going through. Sitting in an elegantly appointed room on Ocean Avenue, its fine furnishings and carpets and curtains dimmed by the last days of an old man taking his time to die, Muggins was insulated against what most people around the world, and many dogs conscripted into war service, were going through just then, more than two years away from the war's end. Perhaps he lay on W.J. Roper's bed (as Queen Victoria's Spitz Turi had done in the queen's last hours some fifteen years earlier) at Osborne House, Roper's hand on his back, Muggins gazing at his master with keen brown eyes that seemed to look not at you, but *into* you. Neither the middle-class housewife on Gorge Road nor the pampered pooch in Oak Bay could have imagined how much their worlds would change in only a month's time, and how much of that change would depend on the wit and loyalty of a rich man's pet of whom nothing important had thus far been expected, of whom everything that was about love and loyalty would be remembered.[19]

CHAPTER 3

"A Relief to Give"

AS MANY IN 1914 CANADA WOULD DISCOVER, NEWS
of war could penetrate even the most distant parts
of the country, even as it was to pervade the lives of
every Canadian.

Nellie McClung was vacationing in rural Manitoba
when, on August 4, it was announced that Britain had
entered the war declared a week earlier. Apart from
the fact that McClung and her fellow vacationers were
already under the enchanting influence of the quiet
countryside and the promise of nothing more important than tennis or walks in the woods, the very idea of
mobilizing for war was one they could not accept, its
fact one they could not take seriously, at least for the
moment. "When the news of war came, we did not
really believe it!" McClung wrote. "War! That was over!
There had been war, of course, but that had been long
ago, in the dark ages, before the days of free schools
and peace conferences and missionary conventions and
labor unions!"[1]

In general, the war broke over a world mostly aston-
ished that it could even be happening at all, and if this
incredible news burst like bombs in the small sum-
mering communities of rural Canada, it had much the
same effect in quiet, controlled Victoria, so conscious of
the indignity of being thrust into a fuss over anything.

There has always been something comical, grandi-
ose, self-absorbed, remote, strange, and warmly familiar about Victoria, a studied eccentricity that did not go
unnoticed by such of its natives capable of achieving the
necessary distance, not to mention the daring, to write
about it. "You can't catalogue Victoria," explained Ann
de Bertrand Lugrin, a local writer of fiction and nonfic-
tion who would one day have a painter called Emily
Carr as writing pupil, and who was said to be working
on a biography of Muggins to be published (though
it was not) after his death. Anyone who has lived for
any length of time in the city featured in her article
will understand immediately what Lugrin is driving at,
through a blend of humour and criticism. "[Victoria]
has no place in any of the lists. She's at the top of her
own special column, and there isn't another to compete
with her . . . She's a unique anomaly, an aristocrat, an
autocrat, a democrat and a beloved vagabond." The city
was at once a lover's paradise and a garden fancier's
dream, with roses growing well into December (out-
lasting the afterglow of most summer honeymoons),
where titled refugees from the rules of upper class
British society could be found milking cows on their
dairy farms and yet still pulling rank when required;
where a combination of commercial activity, sometimes
rising to fever pitch, was pitted against a decided call
for genteel quiet which would have done credit to the

Grant Hayter-Menzies

sleepiest neighbourhoods of Bournemouth, England, and the presence of provincial government amidst it all only added to the strange sense of complex societal tensions buttressed against stalwart bureaucracy whose wheels and gears (and varied political agendas) were happiest turning as slowly as possible. Victoria is, perhaps predictably, not all that different today.[2]

Once the initial shock was over, however, the news of war had a galvanizing effect on Victorians, perhaps for the most part because the quiet seaside city was a place of retirement for so many former colonial military officers, whose blood never failed to run hot for a marching military band or any of the military activities that took place in a city that had boasted a major British Royal Navy yard until 1911 and still had a busy armoury just north of downtown.

A singularly effective group, energized by the outbreak of war to emerge from their drawing rooms and kitchens and gardens, were the women of Victoria. If the various strata of Victoria society had mostly kept to themselves before the war, they would discover during it that the only way to get things done was to work together.

Wives of retired military officers and former colonial officials would have been well equipped to organize a response to war, simply because their whole lives had revolved around a domestic sphere in which delegating authority and giving orders to subordinates were as accepted as having the door held open when entering a restaurant or club. They were versed in the planning of charity fêtes and the summoning and marshalling of voluntary human resources to staff them. They were also women who were, for the most part, of a powerfully patriotic persuasion. And, of course, many of them were mothers. I remember, as an American boy during the last years of the Vietnam War, telling my mother I was afraid they would come get me and send me into battle, and how she assured me she would drive me and my brother over the border to Canada before she would let that happen. She also told me something else. "There would be no wars," she said, "if mothers were in charge. Few women, lined up behind their sons on either side of a battlefield, would want to see another mother's child killed by hers, let alone to see her child killed by another woman's son." This was not a concept of which women in the Great War were unaware. As early as late 1914, just after the Great War began, a song, supported by the pacifist movement, became famous in the United States, the refrain of which went:

> I didn't raise my boy to be a soldier,
> I brought him up to be my pride and joy.
> Who dares to place a musket on his shoulder,
> To shoot some other mother's darling boy?
> Let nations arbitrate their future troubles,
> It's time to lay the sword and gun away.
> There'd be no war today,
> If mothers all would say,
> "I didn't raise my boy to be a soldier."[3]

Admittedly, an American woman and a Commonwealth woman, following outbreak of the war, would naturally have different if not opposing viewpoints on the conflict and what was required of them by armies in need of soldiers. How many Canadian women, feeling torn about letting their sons go to war, drowned out by the theme of sacrifice for the greater good, smothered their own reservations about sending their sons to shoot some other mother's boy by getting deeply involved in war work? There are many more reasons behind the movement than simple patriotism. Long hours of war work dulled the pain of fear and loss, and often moved women in Canada to carry out complicated and stressful but rewarding work at home—not as nurses at the front—to support men in battle. Roused by the threat to all they held dear, Victoria's small and remote corner of the pink map of colonial Great Britain in North America identified needs and mobilized to meet them. Women in Nellie McClung's refined feminine social circle in Manitoba were no less responsive. "In less than a week we were collecting for a hospital ship to be the gift of Canadian women," she wrote. "The message was read out in church one afternoon, and volunteer collectors were asked for. So successful were these collectors all over Canada that in a few days word came to us that enough money had been raised, and that all moneys collected then could be given to the Belgian Relief Fund. The money had simply poured in—it was a relief to give!"[4]

"A relief to give" was a concept which many women embraced, as they were unable to participate in war aside from raising funds for relief and providing their husbands, or sons, or fathers with encouragement from the safe sidelines at home. Not only was work for the cause a way to help keep up their side in the war, it also helped distract them from the ever-present and growing worry about the outcome, for loved ones and for their nation, of this world conflict, a circumstance that was true for the women left behind in all nations involved in the Great War—indeed, for most women in most of the wars known to history.

Muggins's first appearance with his new guardian Beatrice, as donation collection dog for a tag day appeal in support of the Italian Red Cross, appears in the *Daily Colonist* on August 6, 1916.

The appeal was organized by Mrs. Charlotte Pendray, whose husband Herbert came from the BAPCO Paint family (his ancestral home was the towered Queen Anne Pendray mansion in the Inner Harbour, now the Pendray Inn and Teahouse).

The linear fashions of the Great War and post-war periods made Mrs. Pendray—a tall, stately woman, like the similarly shaped Queen Mary—look even more so, a ship's figurehead come to life. And like a figurehead, Charlotte Pendray swept high through the waves of Victoria society on a tide of good works. But then, where the Canadian Red Cross was concerned, the energy and intellect of women was embedded in the very fabric of the organization and everything it carried out during the Great War.

"When Canadians went to fight in South Africa in 1899," writes Sarah Glassford, "the CRCS [Canadian Red Cross Society] Executive Committee went looking for women, appealing to the National Council of Women of Canada (NCWC) for help." As early as August 1914, in the first days after war was declared, it was Canadian women, she adds, who flocked to the Red Cross. One of these women was Adelaide Plumptre, an

Oxford graduate in her early forties who was the wife of the rector of Toronto's St. James Anglican Cathedral and mother of two small children. Adelaide was a woman who got things done. With teaching experience at Havergal College for girls, Adelaide turned her powerfully organized mind—she was described as "an executive genius"—to the Girl Guides, the YWCA, and other organizations where education, health, and patriotism were deemed the saviours of civilization. Which is why she wrote to the Red Cross Society in September 1914, enquiring regarding the enrolment of women among their ranks, the better to effect "assistance which the ladies were desirous of giving." As Glassford writes, with this enquiry began a relationship with the Canadian Red Cross of thirty years' duration, with Adelaide serving as president of the Ontario Division CRCS in the years following the Great War; she would be the first voting female member of the Executive Committee. "Her arrival [in the CRCS] heralded the advent of a rationalized outwork production system for Red Cross supplies the likes of which had never before been seen in Canada," writes Glassford. Adelaide was merely acting on a motivating set of core beliefs, which were not unlike those of nursing pioneer Florence Nightingale: that an organized and efficient methodology could achieve anything; and a core belief of working equine welfare reformer Dorothy Brooke (1883–1955) in Egypt, in which compassion gave her the authority to interfere in any situation whose critical need required it, if the work that needed doing was to get done and get done properly. Seeing Adelaide's example, the women of Canada sat up, listened, and joined in:

... women were the heart and soul of the organization, holding dominion over branch-and-auxiliary-level activity. It was they who organized bake sales, knitted garments, sewed and rolled bandages, held benefit concerts and afternoon teas, and canvassed their neighbourhoods and churches ... Women's tangible, caring work for the CRCS encouraged a clear gender-based division of labour: as several Calgarians pointed out, it was only fair since women were doing the hands-on work, men should finance it.[5]

It can come as no surprise, then, that women were behind virtually all fundraising activities, with the Red Cross and several other charitable organizations aiding the war effort, throughout the time of war.

The first Red Cross Tag Day in Victoria was held on October 21, 1915. This type of fundraising event was very much as it sounds: in exchange for donations made to the Red Cross by passersby solicited by volunteers in the streets, donors were given a tag proving they had made the gift, a bit like a winning ribbon, though not as colourful. "The Red Cross heals the wounds of the world," stated one advertisement published in the days before the sale. "Who among us, living here in prosperity and security, can thoughtlessly neglect or selfishly refuse to GIVE TO OUR UTMOST? Give Freely and Gladly."[6]

Give people did, but to take advantage of that largesse a great deal of organization was required to make a tag day work its magic.

Businesses in the downtown area had to be identified as potential stations for volunteers to sell tags to the public, then contacted and their support verified.

Men from the 50th Regiment Gordon Highlanders of Canada, headquartered at the newly built Bay Street Armoury, got involved as well; like the mostly female volunteers at the tagging stations, they were positioned at street corners and other public spaces apt to reach the most passersby, to advertise and perhaps provide the weight of military approbation to the taggers' work.

There were a number of obstacles to overcome, not least the weather, which in Victoria was not always reliably good for business. Another major one was the role of women in the war effort. The world of the Great War was one which had still not broken free, despite the brief intervening era of Edwardian social freedoms, of the restrictive spell of the Victorian age, in which males dictated the roles women were meant to fill as wives and mothers, for whom the privacy of the home ordained the proper stage for their entire lives. Should, could, would a lady show herself on a public street in an attitude of appearing to sell something to the general public? Many in Victoria did, led by society doyennes like Charlotte Pendray, who for the Italian Red Cross Tag Day cited for especial praise "two little mites, who could not have been more than 4 or 5 years of age, who said that their mothers had sent them to help." So children, in the Victorian sense meant to be seen and not heard, were also escaping the confines of the nursery or home garden and doing their part for the war effort. And among the human mites were three canine ones whose efforts are listed in dollars and cents: Beatrice Woodward's Lulu and Muggins, and a Boston bull terrier called Peter whose guardian was Mrs. H.R. Duce. The three dogs collected a total of $116.75.[7]

It's hard to believe, looking at these impressive donations, that just a little over two years earlier, the eight dogs belonging to members of the Gonzales chapter of the IODE had raised only a total of sixty dollars for the war effort. It's possible this small amount, and the failure of canine collectors to be used again to raise funds, can be explained by the fact that even in late 1914 many people believed (as did many in the military) that the war would be over by Christmas; it was a one-off show of patriotism and collecting donations for a valuable cause of temporary nature.

By 1916, however, when Muggins came on the scene, the world had been at war for twenty-four months. With no end in sight and casualties dominating the daily news in all corners of the empire, the determination to help in any way possible broadened the scope and creativity of fundraising, if only to continue the dream that the conflict would end soon.

That dogs could be incredibly valuable to the war effort—a revelation already acted upon by the German and French military—was demonstrated in 1916 when British command approved their general use on the battlefield. They had finally been convinced by Lt. Col. Edwin Hauteville Richardson, a thin, angular man on whom a uniform seemed to hang as neatly as if arranged over a valet stand, of an idea he had considered vital to military purposes years prior to the Great War: to take advantage of a dog's innate desire to please its master and to be rewarded for an action at that master's direction. This was carried out with a discipline little different from that expected of organizing human forces by training dogs to serve as ancillary members of ambulance companies—carrying medical supplies in saddlebags over their backs, for example—or to bring food and water to men unable to leave their trenches, or most controversially, to be sent through a hail of shot and shell across battlefields of bomb-gouged mud laced with barbed wire, their every move followed by sharpshooters who rarely missed, to carry in a canister around their necks dispatches that, if run successfully, could save whole regiments pinned down by enemy fire, or alert artillery to direct fire at specific zones, and a myriad of other messenger tasks considered too danger-ous for human runners.

"At first there were many sceptics," wrote Richardson, "but as the barrage form of attack became part of the army system, the casualties among [human] runners increased at a terrible rate. Could the dogs take their place? Would they face shell-fire? Could they be depended on?" As Richardson noted, the answer to all of the above was a resounding yes. "They did their duty nobly," he added, "often over land surfaces impossible of traverse by man, and thus saved countless lives—not only the lives of runners, but also those of individual units whose urgent messages they carried." Richardson was fully aware of the poignancy of a faithful though terrified animal running for its trainer, and its life, through a war zone. An Australian officer once marvelled to the colonel at his first glimpse of a messenger-dog in action on the western front. The landscape was a filthy soup of mud, manure, and human and animal remains. "He saw it first coming from the direction of the front-line trenches," recalled Richardson. "The little creature was running along, hopping, jumping, and plunging, and with the most obvious concentration of purpose. He could not imagine what it was doing until it came near and he saw the message-carrier on its neck. As the dog sped past he noticed the earnest expression in its face." The dog was not the popular Airedale or the larger hounds so often used for this purpose, but a goateed black and tan Welsh terrier, not a lot bigger than Muggins.[8]

Parallel to this wartime employment of dogs on the battlefield was another kind of use which had been in place throughout the reign of Queen Victoria, and one with which Beatrice and other Canadian women of English origins would have been familiar: the tradition of dogs collecting for charity, centred mostly around London and the Home Counties (Berkshire, Buckinghamshire, Essex, Hertfordshire, Kent, Surrey, and Sussex).

There were two types of collecting dogs, according to author Jan Bondesen. "Some were privately owned dogs, trained to carry a sign and a collecting box on their back," writes Bondesen. These dogs could be hired by people collecting (or appearing to be collecting) for a charity: "Takings were probably better if the sign on the animal's back said 'For the Red Cross orphanage' or some other charitable endeavour of interest to the public."[9]

These dogs could be accompanied on their rounds, or simply taken to a public space where people foregathered for shopping or other purposes, or to train stations, with their constant flow of humanity, and allowed to wander at will. According to Bondesen, groups of these dogs were owned by some of the charities concerned and were stationed in particular railway stations. "These railway dogs became quite an institution in Victorian and Edwardian life," he writes.

Grant Hayter-Menzies

> The dogs collecting at London's major stations
> became celebrities: notices of their activities were
> published in the *Times* and other newspapers, and
> they featured on numerous postcards. Many of them
> were stuffed after death, to continue collecting for
> their charities.[10]

One of the best known of these dogs was Station Jim of Slough, a large town located twenty miles west of London in Berkshire. Born in the late 1880s, Jim was a stray who then was taken in by the station to be trained to collect donations for the Great Western Railway Widows and Orphans Fund. In his short time wandering the platform wearing his collections boxes strapped to his back, Jim collected the modern equivalent of almost £3,000 for his charity, and he is still collecting donations. He died in 1894, and his body was given to a taxidermist who preserved Jim looking much as he had during his years of collecting on the station platform: nose alert, eyes (though glass) focused on the next potential donor. He is still in his plate glass case at Slough Station, with a placard describing his history and a slot for coins, which commuters continue to donate in his name.[11]

Euston Station, near Regent's Park in London, had two famous collecting dogs. One of these, a Newfoundland cross called Brum, became a favourite of travelling royalty, once accepting a sovereign from King George V himself. "With a little tin box on his back he trotted up and down the station," wrote Ernest Harold Baynes, "barked to attract the attention of his victims, and then shook hands with them if they dropped a coin." By the first year of the war, Brum had collected some $8,000 for charity.[12]

Brum's part collie successor, Roy, was as renowned for refusing to leave the station even after he had been retired to a comfortable home as he was for collecting thousands of pounds for charity. According to one account, Roy's attempts to run away always brought him back to the train station, where he continued trying to solicit donations. Finally convinced to take it easy, Roy died in retirement in October 1925.[13]

It makes sense that the women of the IODE, being of English origin, would have had at least a passing familiarity with the idea of the collection dog, and that in so "English" a place as Victoria, the concept would catch on with little fanfare beyond that always attending the involvement of animals in human endeavours—dogs collecting for charity were obviously no anomaly or they would have surely been noted as such in the Victoria press.

According to a source dating from after Muggins's death, he and a fellow white Spitz called his mate, Lulu, were first taken on collecting trips through the Woodwards' Gorge Road West neighbourhood, and then into downtown, by two children—one of them likely Willie Woodward, the other his playmate-cousin. Money raised was donated to the Red Cross. "Finally the Red Cross authorities asked Muggins's owner to let his [sic] dog be stationed in a booth where he could continue his work more easily." Children played a significant role in the beginning of Muggins's career and they would do so long after its end.[14]

Grant Hayter-Menzies

Muggins's efforts, through Beatrice, were immediately valuable to the war effort but, unfortunately, not immune to the sticky tentacles of municipal bureaucracy. In October 1916, Beatrice and Muggins became figures of especial and not entirely benign interest on the part of a Victoria councillor.

Ironically, because Muggins had already raised $300 (around $5,600 Canadian in 2020) in his first few months of collecting, this achievement made the local press, which is how he came to council's attention. Council concluded that Muggins was not collecting under the auspices of proper authority, implying Beatrice might not direct the donations as she had declared she would do—a technicality without malice, but a charge that must have stung. Beatrice was required to appear before council with a petition requesting permission for Muggins and her son Willie to continue collecting, provided she could obtain endorsements from three charitable societies.

However insulted she may have been (and rightly so), Beatrice cooperated in every way. As she wrote, "I should like to know if I could get a permit that would be good at any time, to be used by my dog 'Muggins' and my little boy Willie, so that they could collect on tag days or any special occasions."[15] With a speed that suggests understandable dismay that Beatrice's and Muggins's efforts should have brought on this attention in the first place, three prominent societies quickly stepped forward to vouch for their bona fides: the Red Cross, the Blue Cross, and the Returned Soldiers Fund.

Canada had partnered with the British Red Cross in 1865, but it was Dr. George Ryerson who, during the Northwest Rebellion twenty years later, raised the first makeshift Red Cross flag, and helped found the Canadian branch in 1896. The Victoria Red Cross held its first official tag day in October 1915. Women volunteers, assisted by the Gordon Highlanders, raised the considerable sum of $5,000 for the Red Cross.[16]

The Blue Cross (not to be confused with the health insurance provider for humans) was founded as Our Dumb Friends Animal League in London, England, in 1896.

Originally meant to support veterinary care for working horses on the streets of London, the Blue Cross expanded scope to provide care and support for horses during the Balkan Wars that preceded the Great War. They aided animals conscripted in the latter as well as the Second World War, and in 1945 helped bring dogs back to the UK to join the servicemen whom they had befriended in battle zones, echoing the work done by the Royal Society for the Prevention of Cruelty to Animals during the Great War and by other charities today.[17]

The Returned Soldiers Fund is inextricably linked to the Reverend Arthur de Brissac Owen, who, in addition to the three charities that vouched for Muggins's credibility, wrote a letter to council himself in support of the dog's charitable endeavours.

In the November 19, 1972, edition of the *Daily Colonist*, Vivienne Chadwick related how she began her piece as a belated tribute to Rev. Owen, only to find that it turned into a double tribute to him and to Muggins.

Born in 1869 in Blackheath, Kent, Rev. Owen owed his middle name to Huguenot ancestors who, fleeing religious persecution in France, found safety and commercial opportunity in London. Employed in Alberta as a missionary to Indigenous communities, Rev. Owen found his teaching routine leavened with adventure. His daughter Mildred Hughes recalled her father dealing coolly with a flood that swamped the lower floor of their home, in which a pregnant guest of the family had just then entered labour, all the while herding his family, the guest, and livestock to higher ground. As one would expect, he had a good sense of humour. When parents of his students accused him of poisoning their sons, after he'd washed the boys' mouths with soap following a streak of foul language from the latter, he ate most of a bar to demonstrate it was harmless; his audience was astounded, while Owen's family saw the real consequences later on at home. On settling in Victoria, Rev. Owen, an inveterate volunteer, "covered the city on his bicycle on his errands of mercy," miraculously avoiding being killed in traffic as he greeted everyone he knew along the way; for years of Christmas mornings, he played Santa Claus to ill children at Jubilee Hospital, handing out gifts and cheer before hurrying home in time to have breakfast with his own children. After the outbreak of war in 1914, Rev. Owen solicited thousands of dollars in donations for needy families, "hunting down" every wealthy parishioner and many outside his jurisdiction. "He hounded the fuel companies," his daughter remembered, "for free winter coal for old ladies with heating problems."[18]

Rev. Owen was especially concerned about the welfare of returned soldiers. In an ideal world, these men, having served their country and risked their lives to do so, would have been welcomed back after the war with not only open arms but with jobs and places to live as they resumed life with families they had not seen for several years or started new families or simply new lives. But such was not the case. As Tim Cook, writing of the "new and vibrant society" formed among soldiers from disparate origins living through the same hell of war, so movingly writes, "Would the secrets of survival resonate beyond the deadly trenches, where so much of the culture had been spawned, and would this culture still matter to the soldiers as they returned to their civilian lives?"[19]

Rev. Owen realized that the men who were returning were the same men who had left and yet were wholly changed by experiences in which facing death was a daily ritual. He also knew the limitations of local, provincial, and federal government to address the needs of returned veterans, thus volunteer organizations had a vital role filling in where they could (an issue raising its head again in Victoria where the homeless are concerned). He organized transportation for the men from the dock, where he met and greeted every one, and if they had no place to go, he found them one. To help pay for these veterans' expenses, Rev. Owen and a group of Victoria ladies organized a flower guild. In season, flowers from gardens all over Victoria were made up by the guild ladies into bouquets, nosegays, and boutonnieres, which were sold at the docks to arriving or departing visitors. Funds from the proceeds were used to provide loans to returning veterans to help them set themselves up in civilian life again.

This, then, is where Muggins entered Rev. Owen's life and his work. The 1972 *Daily Colonist* article includes a photo of Rev. Owen standing beside his bicycle, gazing with a smile of pure delight at Muggins, who sits up on his donation table near the Empress Hotel, appearing

Grant Hayter-Menzies

to smile back at the clergyman. They became a team, with flowers gathered by the guild sold from Muggins's stand near the Empress Hotel and the funds counted and distributed by Rev. Owen, to the point where they became as inseparable in the minds of press and public as Muggins and the soldiers who loved him. Chadwick writes at the end of her feature on Owen, "I am entirely sure that a man of the Rev. Arthur Owen's calibre would be quite happy to share with his friend and co-worker this late limelight, this long-delayed salute."[20]

The good reverend's letter on behalf of Muggins's work, so soon after he started it, stood him in good stead with Mayor Alex Stewart and council, as it would do over the course of the next three years.

Having at last been cleared for his continued work by Victoria city council, and with the backing of respected local charities and the beloved Rev. Owen, Muggins's most serious efforts, starting in autumn 1916, can be said to have begun.

Right from the beginning, thanks to the flower guild's work on the docks, Muggins was also on the front lines with them, when one of the era's great ocean liners, the *Empress of Asia*, previously conscripted into war (and to be conscripted again, fatally as it happened, for the next world war), was released back to its owners to resume transpacific travel.

In the first week of November 1916, Muggins is described as being already well known among the liners docking at Victoria Harbour, and we know he did this work alone, for the most part. (A year later, travellers who had heard about Muggins would actively seek him out, not just to put coins in his collection tins but to meet him, as one would a human celebrity. One of these visitors to Victoria, prominent Australian clothing manufacturer James L.G. Law, sent a Muggins postcard, given to him after he'd donated, back home to his daughter in Melbourne, noting that Muggins—"this bow wow"—was there to greet them on their arrival in Victoria.) One witness to Muggins's methods was American Samuel Brown Kirkwood, a lifelong animal lover, future president of the American University of Beirut, and a prime example of the kind of humans who were drawn to Muggins.

Born in Seattle in 1907, Kirkwood had had a connection to animals from his earliest years, according to his daughter Diana. She recalled how, in her childhood, the family dog fell ill with canine encephalitis, a mostly fatal neurological condition. Kirkwood nursed the dog day and night for a month and a half, after veterinarians had given up, and administered a human antiseizure drug, Dilantin, with such success that the dog recovered. This desperate experiment, says Kirkwood's daughter, contributed to what became inoculation for canine distemper, benefiting countless numbers of dogs in future.[21]

Kirkwood was visiting from Seattle when he first met the famed white Spitz of Victoria's Inner Harbour. "The minute the gangplank touched the pier," wrote Kirkwood, "Muggins would jump down from his stand . . . and [alone] run on board to collect what money he could." The little dog made a beeline first for the card rooms. Past experience, Kirkwood presumed, led him to realize that he would not only find many passengers there—much as one would find, in pre-pandemic days, plenty of passengers in the casino of any given cruise ship today—but also easy pickings when it came to collecting donations. Kirkwood clearly saw Muggins in action: his first line of attack was to distract the players, circling the table and nudging knees as he passed. Should that method not produce results, Muggins would begin barking, jumping up so the coins in his collection boxes rattled noisily. "If this method of advertisement did not secure the attention of the players, which was not often," Kirkwood wrote, "he did not hesitate to jump upon one of the tables and remain there till all had contributed."[22]

A mystery in most accounts of Muggins at work is the persistent incredulity that he did not require a handler in his collection work.

This remains a mystery today. We know he had once been the pet of an elderly man who was ill for most of the time Muggins was with him. With the Roper Hulls, Muggins would have been taken for walks by a servant, or by Mrs. Roper Hull, but his life in Oak Bay had been circumscribed, quiet, controlled. After Beatrice involved him in collection work, Muggins's ability to not only set forth on a task amid crowds of strangers, by himself, does not lend itself easily to explanation. Had Beatrice or someone else trained him, and what did that training involve? If there was such training available in Victoria, why do we not hear of it in connection to the other collection dogs or, indeed, in newspaper articles from the war period?

Preponderance of evidence suggests that Muggins only came into Beatrice's care shortly after the death of

William Roper Hull in early August 1916; not long following, Muggins was collecting for the Italian Tag Day at the Empress Hotel. My guess is that if there was any training, it was minimal.

Knowing Muggins's background, what would make more sense is that the tricks he is on record as performing on command—sitting up to "beg," turning around, barking on cue—were a small sample of his learning capacity and a large part of what attracted people, and their donations, to him.

Perhaps Beatrice and Rev. Owen had taken him down to the docks one day to sell flowers, noticed the interest in him from visitors off the ship, and managed to show him what they wanted: that he, wearing a harness with donation cups on either side—two Fry's cocoa containers, painted white with the Red Cross or other charities' emblems affixed—go aboard with Beatrice, and solicit passengers to drop coins in his tins.

The dropping of coins in the tins, with a pleasant clink, is known to have excited the dog, who was also seen to show dismay when soundless (if far more generous) gifts of paper cash were pushed through his collection tins' apertures. Trotting about with the rattling tins at either side, Muggins learned the more coins, the happier Beatrice and Rev. Owen when the tins were turned out and the cash counted. He must have made an association between the weight of the coins with greater pleasure expressed by these humans, and so keenly pursued getting people to drop coins in.

A wartime newsreel from about 1918 captures Muggins's delight: as a passing visitor drops in a coin and pats Muggins on the head, he whirls around on his stand, white plume of his tail whipping in the breeze.

The frequent description of Muggins as being clever, smart, and bright, were not simply catchwords to make for interesting articles, but truthful observations of his awareness of his duties and the intelligence with which he carried them out. Which makes it easy to imagine how he could go aboard these ocean liners alone, and get back off with his filled containers, without being trampled or getting lost or ending up an unintended stowaway. (The one time Muggins is known to have sailed forth on a ship without Beatrice's permission was when a sailor couldn't bear to let him go; a tender was sent out to retrieve him.)

Muggins was soon carrying not just his donation tins but also a cache of postcards bearing his image. Perhaps Beatrice had had these made after city council gave her and Muggins permission to continue their work. If so, she wasted no time. These postcards would come to encompass not only a formal standing pose (and sometimes sitting up to beg), with a Union Jack hanging behind Muggins and tied, in the form of a scarf, to his collection harness, and the Canadian Red Ensign under his feet, but also posed outdoor shots of Muggins with soldiers beside an ambulance, sitting with nurses and recovering wounded soldiers on porch steps at Esquimalt Military Hospital, and most notably with Gen. Sir Arthur Currie at the Empress Hotel. As Muggins's collecting totals crested the $1,000 range, a stamp was made to use on the cards: MUGGINS' VICTORIA BC. COLLECTED OVER $3,000, for example, the total having to be revised often.

So far as we know, the only other dog who came close to Muggins's collection success and popularity, Peter the bull terrier, belonging to Mrs. H.R. Duce, did not have such postcards circulated, though photographs appeared in the local newspaper. (He was said to have been taken after the end of the Great War to California, where he appeared in movies—but confirming this has proved problematic.)

From the start, Muggins's life was a busy daily regimen almost comparable to that of a human holding down a full-time job, much of it accomplished on his own among strangers and crowds, street-side and ship-side. And he made it work.

A brief film clip from 1920 of activity aboard the *Empress of Asia*, as the ship docks in Japan, gives an idea of what Muggins had to contend with at the Victoria docks and on board the ship.

The Empresses, as the *Empress of Asia*, *Empress of Russia*, and *Empress of Japan* were known, outpaced larger Pacific liners by the mere fact of their modern design and their speed. With the fate of the *Titanic* in mind, the Empresses were the first to be designed so that four entire containers could flood without the ship sinking, giving more time to rescue passengers. The ships could accommodate 284 first-class passengers, 100 second-class, and over 800 in what was termed "Oriental steerage" from the many Chinese people brought to serve in the Great War in France. The first-class reception and dining rooms were designed with up-to-date elegance in mind. The *Empress of Asia*'s smoking room, with its carved wood panelling left in its natural colour, was considered a triumph of ocean liner decor for the time.[23]

One question that may occur to the reader, as it did to the writer, is why ocean liners were still plying the Pacific Ocean during the war. In fact, Muggins's boarding of the *Empress of Asia* was something of a fluke

Grant Hayter-Menzies

of luck, because all three Empresses were requisitioned for the war effort, with the *Asia* being requisitioned even before actual war began. Like the other Empresses, the *Asia* had an adventurous career, from summer 1914 to fall 1915, when she was released back to her owners, just in time for Muggins's fundraising visits over the next three years. She was active first in the Yellow Sea, then the Red Sea; she patrolled waters for German ships, briefly sailing alongside the infamous *Emden* at some ten miles apart. By the time the *Asia* was released from naval commission at Mumbai, India, on October 22, 1915, she had travelled a total of 64,024 miles.[24]

In a *Daily Colonist* article from a little over a year later, Muggins was described in action during his *Empress of Asia* visits. He apparently left few areas of the ship unexplored. "Muggins travels alone most of the time," wrote the reporter, though we know from other sources that Beatrice usually accompanied him unless there was some reason, such as wartime security measures, that she was forbidden to go aboard.

Nothing seemed to stop Muggins. As the little white dog with his collection tins jangling on his harness became more familiar, crew and passengers both looked forward to seeing him as soon as they had docked. He was seen to be more than ordinarily responsive to attention. Even when trotting through a crowd, he would catch his name or a called "Here, boy!" and come immediately to the person addressing him. Muggins had, in addition, an endearing habit of barking every time donations were placed in his collection tins, and would wait patiently, gazing up at the donor, while he or she selected a postcard of the dog from a holder fixed to the harness, as souvenir of the gift and the experience.[25]

Muggins's draw on the public's attention is clear from newspaper accounts, but it is even easier to understand in a brief newsreel clip from 1918, now part of the Royal British Columbia Archives.

A stand was built for Muggins to sit on, and was placed at the corner of Government and Belleville Streets, a busy confluence of both arriving ship passengers and the cross-currents of daily foot traffic, where the Parliament Buildings looked across Belleville Street at the Empress Hotel. Muggins's platform had grown by this time from a table, on which the dog lay, to a little pavilion, square in shape, with a striped roof, and at its back a cloth panel on which were pinned postcards of Muggins, posing by himself in various settings, or with wounded soldiers or nurses and ambulance staff and, occasionally, officers.

A sign hanging at the front of the table described what was going on: MY NAME IS MUGGINS, it began, and below listed his current age, who he was collecting for—at the time of filming, it was the Red Cross, the emblem of which was on his collection tins as well as on various objects on the table—and how much he had raised to date. There was also a firm disclosure that he was not being forced to do this. Such information was meant to address a concern which had begun with focus on abused working equines, but which by now took in the welfare of a broad spectrum of animals, interest in which was so general among the population it would have been unthinkable to present Muggins at work without stating the precise conditions of that work.

The Prevention of Cruelty to Animals Act had been legislated in 1895, and by 1901 there were branches of the Society for the Prevention of Cruelty to Animals in every major urban area in British Columbia, including Victoria. By the time of the Great War, it would not have been easy putting a dog on a table to solicit donations without explaining to a good many passersby that he was not being forced or undergoing suffering of any kind in the process—though, of course, this is all from the viewpoint of the humans putting him there and explaining his situation on his behalf.

That Muggins enjoyed the attention, however, is clear from the newsreel. The clip begins with Muggins jumping up the three feet needed to sit atop the table, no small feat for a short-legged Spitz. Once he is there, Beatrice, in summer whites, fastens his harness and collection tins around his middle, and then he is filmed doing tricks: sitting back on his haunches and waving his paws, a Muggins speciality that is captured in a number of photographs. At that point the camera pulls back and we see Muggins sitting in his pavilion as waves of pedestrians pass before him. We see an elegantly dressed gentleman, evidently just off his ship, stride past the pavilion, turn on his heel, look at Muggins, and come back to him, where he drops a donation in his tin and gives his head a pat. Others walk straight for him. At times, between his wagging white fluff of tail and the reaching hands, it's difficult to see him. Two young girls in white eyelet dresses and silk hairbows approach him and he seems to know them, turning away from his audience to greet them and be petted. From this short glimpse alone, it is easy to see why the amount he collected had to be revised so often on his sign that every photo of him with it shows a different and larger amount. And it is easy to see why he touched passing strangers to such a degree they couldn't help but leave a donation for his cause, and why for the "frequent fliers" who regularly booked passage on the Empress liners, the sight of the little white dog with his collection tins was something many looked forward to as they watched Victoria Harbour hove into view across the water.[26]

CHAPTER 4

"Who Could Resist That Little Spitz With the Imploring Eyes?"

"PERHAPS YOU THINK THAT YOU CAN'T DO ANY-thing to help with the war," intoned the Canadian children's magazine *King's Own* in August 1918. But there was no need to wait until one reached fighting age to play a role in the conflict. In terms that would have been familiar to children who went regularly to church, "You can fight the Germans by fighting the enemies inside your heart."[1]

There were children much closer to the setting of the Great War who were dealing with the very real possibility that they would be deprived of home, and possibly life and limb, at any hour. I knew one of them, an elderly lady in Victoria who, as a small child in London, remembered the war in distinct, frightening detail.

"I was awakened one night, out of a sound sleep," Cecy Baldwin (1913–2009) told me in the quiet calm of her Esquimalt garden almost a century later, "and told I must come downstairs, as there were zeppelins overhead." When we think of German aerial bombing campaigns, we think of the Blitz early in the Second World War, which devastated so much of London, with forces capable of killing, injuring, and making homeless thousands of people in a single raid. But the Great War's more small-scale German air raids over England managed to rain considerable hell down on London and other targeted locations. "What was so haunting about the zeppelins," Cecy told me, "was how quiet they were. Their approach, I mean. As my nurse hurried me downstairs and through the garden—our destination was the basement of a neighbour's house, considered safer than our own—my mother clutching a few valuables, I remember hearing the strange clanking of the propellers. In that dark sky, in a state of fear, to see nothing but to hear that skeletal clanking of gears, and to know that death floated over our heads . . . I can never forget it."[2]

No child in Canada experienced such looming terror, but it can be argued that few did not have an uncle, brother, cousin, or father who had crossed the Atlantic to fight for king and country against the juggernaut of imperial Germany or, lacking these, did not have friends at school with relatives male or female who were somehow involved in the conflict. Canadian children were extraordinarily active in work that while segregated between the sexes (though occasionally boys could be found learning to knit socks for soldiers when they found out that wounded returned veterans were lying in hospital beds doing the same), raised funds from a variety of means. There was, for example, a

Children's Self-Denial Fund described by a school inspector in Revelstoke, British Columbia, which required children to "contribute for patriotic purposes not less than 5 cents and not more than 25 cents each month . . . saved or earned by themselves."[3]

This was in 1916, when twenty-five cents Canadian had close to five dollars Canadian in purchasing power today. As Susan Fisher writes, "Were all Canadian children happy to knit socks and give up their hard-earned pennies?" Probably not; that's human nature. She notes that there must have been no fewer such children then as there would be now, if required to make the same sacrifices of their time and saved earnings from chores. During the war, however, "it would have been a hard case indeed who could still hold out when reminded of how men—even their own fathers, brothers, cousins, or uncles—were dying on the battlefields." Deny that quarter, and be reminded of a male relative fighting in the trenches, perhaps captured as a POW—or his life sacrificed on the field of war.[4]

Victoria's children seem to have been especially active in fundraising for the war effort. In 1918, in just one example, children in Victoria collected almost $4,000, close to $60,000 in 2020 values, by gathering up waste paper, which was then sold to benefit the Red Cross and other charities, much of the work done through the children's schools.[5]

We have seen how Muggins's first known foray into collecting donations for the war effort took place among a small army of children for the 1916 Italian Red Cross Tag Day. This was not a one off. We know from Beatrice's petition to Victoria city council to allow Muggins to collect donations that her adopted son Willie accompanied the dog on his rounds. Another example is known as well. In 1913, the Baines family—Herbert Baines, his wife, and daughter, Kathleen, then three years old—emigrated to Canada from England, settling on a farm near Calgary. They were there only a year when, at outbreak of war in summer 1914, Herbert enlisted to fight. His wife and daughter were moved to Victoria. It is possible that Englishwomen like Beatrice, who had lived in Victoria for a decade at that point, assisted Mrs. Baines in this adjustment to living in a new city after their brief time on the Alberta farm. Mrs. Baines soon became involved in the effort to fundraise for the war. Daughter Kathleen, then a child of about five (in 1915), began to assist also, becoming Muggins's sidekick as he collected in downtown Victoria. Kathleen's daughter, Christine O'Brien, remembered her mother telling her how Muggins was given dollar bills for the cause. The Baines' life in Victoria was to also be of short duration. As with the case of Harry Woodward, who first came to Canada, enlisted and fought in the war, and returned to England, Mrs. Baines and seven-year-old Kathleen went back to their native country after Herbert, already weakened from war wounds, died in the Spanish flu pandemic in 1919.[6]

That there were children other than Kathleen Baines involved with Muggins's work is clear from press coverage throughout his collection career. In April 1917, despite inclement weather, about three hundred Victoria women volunteered on behalf of the Women's Auxiliary to the Military Convalescent Hospitals to hand out tags to those who donated to the cause. Both Muggins and Peter were with them, and "did valiant work through-out the day," according to the *Daily Colonist*, receiving "numerous subscriptions large and small in their boxes." The reporter noted that children were most eager to give their coins in donation when the dogs were present to receive them. Several cases were described by the volunteers of "'little fellows' who came forward with their contributions and asking for a tag."[7] In May, too, Muggins and Peter proved the star attractions of another successful tag day, with children crowding to see them and make their deposit in their collection tins.[8] And when Muggins and Peter were included in the first Victory Loan Parade, held in downtown Victoria in November 1917, Muggins and Peter were accompanied on their flag-draped float by two little girls, Luella Waage-Mott, daughter of a Lieut. Robert William Waage-Mott, and Norsen Marsden, whose officer father was with the 8th Battalion (Winnipeg).[9]

One of the most touching memories of what Muggins meant to children is that of Jim Ferguson, who was six years old in 1916, the year Muggins's collecting work began. Interviewed in his mid-nineties, Ferguson described what it was like for a little boy to see his father go off to war. "He was part of the Bantam regiment," he recalled of his father, "an infantry group of men who were less than average height . . . My dad joked that being short was an advantage in the trenches." Memories from age six can be fitful and few, particularly for a person closing in on a century of life, but Ferguson never forgot his mother's sadness at seeing her husband off to war. "We stood across the harbour and watched the soldiers marching onto the boat," he recalled. "It was just before Christmas and the band was playing Christmas music." Ferguson and his sister were further disappointed that their mother did not put up a Christmas tree that holiday season. The one memory that stood out above the others, he said, "is that of a little white Spitz dog named Muggins. Across from the present Bay Centre at Fort and Government," Ferguson said, "which was known as the Five Sisters Block, was a burned-out area that had been made into a mock dugout to house the Victoria Red Cross." Built out of logs which had been caulked with mud, according to the method used by British forces on the battlefields of France, the dugout included a sunken area that was trench-like, a mild hint of the conditions prevailing for troops in Europe. Above were hand-lettered signs adjuring passersby to KEEP THE HUN ON THE RUN by purchasing Victory Bonds; the latter were typically sold by soldiers who had been invalided home. Ferguson's mother, he recalled, would take him and his sister downtown to the Red Cross Centre, once or twice per month, where she could get supplies. When young Ferguson was first taken to the dugout, he remembered being met by a woman wearing the uniform of the Red Cross, and how his mother told him that this was like the setting in which his father was surviving at that moment. "That was where we spotted Muggins. He was the cutest dog I'd ever seen," Ferguson said. Because the Ferguson children did not have a dog at home, just being able to touch one, especially so famous a dog as Muggins, was an unforgettable experience. It was just as wonderful, Ferguson said, to see how seriously the dog took his role as fundraiser for the cause. He stood there patiently but keenly, on his table, with his harness and cash pan-niers across his back, looking into the eyes of all who passed. Few could avoid that gaze, or resist it. Ferguson's only misgivings were that nobody could tell him where

Grant Hayter-Menzies

Muggins lived. Where did he sleep, eat? Mrs. Ferguson didn't know, and she was far too harassed by the daily struggles of life running her household on her own, finding enough food for her children, and enough hope to give them about the future, to care much about a dog, however charismatic and cute he was.[10]

Obviously, though, in the mind and heart of an elderly man who had been that little boy, Muggins was more than just a little Red Cross dog. He was a being who cared about other beings, who awakened in the hearts of children and non-children alike a compassion all too often, and rather too indiscriminately, ascribed only to human hearts.

The sheer volume of activity for Muggins on a daily basis is difficult to fully understand or grasp on a real-life scale, because it goes without saying that Muggins left no written record of what his collection work was like for him, and we regretfully do not have any evidence that some enterprising reporter ever tagged along on his route from the docks to downtown Victoria.

This is strange, as we are now well within the era when journalists were adding "animal interest" stories to the pages of daily papers, and when gumshoes were making themselves part of crowds and movements to gauge public opinion on a variety of issues, take the temperature of public perception of politics and politicians, and bring readers past the newsprint page to a more personal understanding (with understandable biases) of issues of the day.

In researching books about war horses and war dogs, I had read articles in which reporters interviewed the animals concerned, or invented conversations among them, in a tradition carried on from Anna Sewell's *Black Beauty, the Autobiography of a Horse*, published in 1895, in which a horse tells of its own life's challenges, tragedies, and joys in a human-centred world. So I decided to make up for the omission by not only tracing Muggins's assumed route, but to take along my dog Freddie.

Like Muggins, Freddie happens to also be a Spitz, though he is black where Muggins was white, and Freddie comes from a very different background to that of his predecessor: he was rescued from a backyard breeder-hoarder by the BCSPCA. Ten years of security and love had not quelled all of Freddie's past trauma, but through us he learned to play with toys, to trust that he would always have food and water, and above all, that he could rely on us to never cause him any harm. Happily, Freddie is as keen and curious as Muggins and, like him, he enjoys a good long walk.

I knew Muggins's initial collecting points consisted of at least four different Victoria locations. There was the harbour causeway, where the liners docked. There was the intersection of Belleville and Government Streets, where his collection stand was placed. There was the front of Wilson's Drug Store, at Government and Fort Streets (now the location of Maison Birks), where he often sat collecting with Beatrice or another volunteer, and sometimes a child minder, keeping him company. Near that was what was called the dugout, a recreated sandbagged trench constructed beside the burned-out ruins of the former Spencer's and Five

Grant Hayter-Menzies

Sisters Block, totally destroyed in 1911 and still undeveloped; Muggins was often there, too.

The destination that most interested me was the Temple Building, at 525 Fort Street, then used as headquarters for the Red Cross. Muggins was often seen there, particularly on one singular occasion involving the police, which we will explore later on.

Lacking any definite information, I could only assume that Beatrice, on Muggins's return from his collecting aboard ship, would see him safely down the gangplank and then send him uptown to the Temple Building to deliver his haul of the coins jingling in his cocoa tins. So Freddie and I started where Oswego Street turns into Belleville, just northwest of the Black Ball Ferry terminal.

I glanced down at Freddie, who is, like Muggins, a sturdy dog, and saw him keenly observing the activity around him as breezes off the strait ruffled his fur. I couldn't imagine leaving him to his devices anywhere, let alone in what even in 1916–1919 was a busy harbour teeming with civilians and sailors, all the streets of downtown a confusion of motor cars and horse-drawn equipages often at cross purposes with one another.

Dogs have a marvellous sense of recall, remembering places, faces, and pathways that they may have only seen a few times and can remember when their human companion has long forgotten. They are also creatures of habit. This is coupled with a homing sense which still astonishes us when we read of a lost dog finding its way back where it came from over many hundreds and even thousands of miles, and over many weeks, months, or years. Having negotiated the crowded decks of an ocean liner, scurrying among a forest of legs and feet, trousers and skirts, with perhaps the captain as his one familiar reference, Muggins would then have had to find his way along sidewalks similarly crowded until he arrived at the Temple Building, a little over two kilometres away.

One hundred and four years later, I allowed Freddie's homing instinct to lead us forth. He had not yet been to the Temple Building, but he, like all dogs, knew how to find the straightest way forward, whatever the ultimate destination.

As if reading my mind—something he does often—Freddie pointed his sharp nose toward Belleville Street, and off we went.

It was a fine day, one of those late spring Victoria afternoons when the clear warmth of the sun is just briefly interrupted by sheets of sharp breezes off the ocean. We were serenaded by birds, barked at by other dogs, greeted by people watering their gardens. We passed apartment houses and condominiums and the lovely quaintness of Victorian, Queen Anne, and Craftsman houses which "progress" had not yet levelled.

Making a right at Belleville, we headed east, past the Black Ball Ferry terminal and the Neptune-festooned façade of Francis Rattenbury's former steamship terminal, now the Robert Bateman Centre. On the other side floated that other Rattenbury masterpiece, the Parliament Buildings, with the statue of Queen Victoria gazing down at us from her granite plinth. Making a left on Government Street, where Muggins's donation stand had been so familiar a sight, we walked north, past the castle-like Empress Hotel, that other site of so many celebrations honouring Muggins during and after the Great War, and then into Victoria's historic business district which, despite the vicissitudes of local politics and the ebb and flow of the local economy, has managed to retain much of the appearance it had when Muggins was alive.

Reaching Fort Street, we turned left, and there we found the Temple Building. It took us, at a leisurely stroll, about forty-five minutes. Muggins probably made it in half that time, if not faster.

Built in 1893 to a design by Samuel Maclure, the Temple Building is a handsome, slightly out of place structure of neat red brick atop a rusticated base of sandstone, its high arched windows looking out at the world like a curious old gentleman with his monocle.[11]

Thirteen stone steps lead from the street entrance up to the second storey, and therein lies a famous tale. The September 1, 1917, edition of the *Daily Colonist* reported that "a lively discussion ensued yesterday at noon in front of the Temple Building headquarters of the Victoria Red Cross Society. One irate citizen wanted to send for the Prevention of Cruelty to Animals, while another insisted it was a case for the licence inspector or the city police."[12]

Muggins had been seen trying to climb this high staircase, weaving from side to side, his donation tins "so filled as to justify the suspicion that he was either intoxicated or criminally overloaded." It turned out that he had just come back from collecting aboard the *Empress of Asia*, whose passengers had been especially generous, to the tune, when all the coins were counted, of over $400 (a little over $8,000 in current Canadian dollars). The concerned citizens saw him trying to get up the stairs with this load; he may have slipped as he proceeded upward, or stopped and stood still under the weight, then tried again, one step at a time, and

I am sure anyone today witnessing the sight would be speed-dialling the BCSPCA as readily as the witnesses a century ago. It is possible these people helped Muggins the rest of the way up to the Red Cross offices, and asked for an explanation, demanding that the heavy tins be removed from the dog's harness. This was done but, to everyone's surprise, "Muggins rapidly recovered and showed much pride in the gratifying results of the morning's work" by jumping and barking, no worse for wear.[13]

I'm not sure, even after a more relaxed walk than busy Muggins ever took from the old CPR steamship terminal, that Freddie, let alone his huffing and puffing middle-aged human, could have made it up those thirteen stone steps with the equivalent of almost double our weight on our backs. How did he do it? As we stood in front of the Temple Building, cars whizzing past, I looked down at Freddie and asked his opinion. He gazed up at me with brown eyes bright with interest, proffering no advice, but happy to be with me.

As Dr. Jeffrey Moussaieff Masson has said, dogs never lie about love. Nor do they ever feel the need to explain (particularly at length, as humans invariably do). Indeed, I'm sure had I asked Muggins the same question, I'd have received the same answer: How did I do it? I don't know. Did I love doing it? Yes!

Andy and Dorothy Hilliard with uncle William Roper Hull at Langmore in Calgary. William R. Hull's love for animals is obvious here; note the white Spitz being held by Hull's niece, Dorothy. Glenbow Archives NA-3918-22

Emmeline Hull, née Banister, was the wife of William Roper Hull. The dog
that appears in this photo bears a strong resemblance to Lulu, the Spitz
pictured in a September 1913 article in Victoria's *Daily Colonist*.
Glenbow Archives NA-3918-17

Langmore, residence of William Roper Hull, Calgary. Built between 1902 and 1905, Langmore remained the home of Emmeline Hull after her husband's death in 1924. This may have also been the birthplace, and briefly the home, of Muggins. Glenbow Archives NC-24-170

William J. Roper of Cherry Creek. Uncle of William Roper Hull, Roper owned the Cherry Creek Ranch near Kamloops, BC. He and wife Edith later moved to Victoria, where they lived in Oak Bay, and Muggins with them. Image H-00494 courtesy of the Royal BC Museum and Archives

Volunteers for Italian Tag Day. This is the first known photograph of Muggins at work as fundraiser in August 1916. Posing in front of the Empress Hotel, Muggins can be seen standing at right, with his mate, Lulu, at left, and Peter, collection dog of Mrs. H.R. Duce, at centre. Image J-02400 courtesy of the Royal BC Museum and Archives

590 Gorge Road West House: The residence of Beatrice and
George Woodward, their adopted son Willie, and dogs Muggins and
Lulu. Saanich Archives CR-114-2006-015-278a

CAMC Soldiers on the *Princess Victoria*. Muggins was often taken aboard ship by soldiers. He can be seen here, with the Empress Hotel in the background, being held by the Rev. Arthur de Brissac Owen as they stand among soldiers of the Canadian Army Medical Corps. Image J-01499 courtesy of the Royal BC Museum and Archives

"MUGGINS"   Victoria, B. C.
Collected Over $3,000

Shortly after Muggins began collecting donations, postcards bearing
his image were exchanged with donors, many of them stamped with his
collected total to date. Author's Collection

POST CARD

VANCOUVER B.C
SEP 28
1 - PM
1917
MADE IN CANADA

$25⁰⁰ FOR $21
HOW?
ASK YOUR B
OR POSTMAS

CANADA POSTAGE
TWO
2 CENTS

CORRESPONDENCE HERE

NAME AND ADDRESS HERE

Victoria
British Columbia
27-9-17.
Dear Wee Poss
We saw this bow
wow today when we arr'd
Love from Mum & Dad

Mrs. Pauline M. Law.
"Drumtochty"
61 Hambleton S
Albert Park
Victoria
Australia

This postcard of Muggins, sent back from Victoria to family in Melbourne, Australia, by James L.G. Law in September 1917, shows the international reach of the little dog's fame. Courtesy of Melissa McLean, granddaughter of James L.G. Law

My name is
MUGGINS
I am six years old
I have collected $13,000 for the Red Cross
I WANT TO GET   HELP THE BOYS WHO
$20,000.   FOUGHT FOR YOU.
I am not chained to my job.
I am just doing my bit
Have you done yours?

Postcard of Muggins on his portable table.
Saanich Archives PR-149-2015-028-002

Postcard of Muggins with the Royal Canadian Reserve.
Saanich Archives PR-149-2015-028-007

Postcard of Muggins with wounded soldiers at Esquimalt Military Hospital. Saanich Archives PR-149-2015-028-008

Postcard of Muggins with two soldiers and a Red Cross ambulance.
Saanich Archives PR-149-2015-028-010

Postcard of Peace Parade with Red Cross float followed by Muggins atop
ambulance. Saanich Archives PR-149-2015-028-012

Postcard of Muggins with Gen. Sir Arthur Currie on the steps of the
Empress Hotel. Saanich Archives PR-149-2015-028-005

THE GREAT EUROPEAN WAR.~~.
Declared·4/8/14·Ended·

"MUGGINS".
A·VICTORIA · COLLECTOR · FOR · THE · FUNDS·
OF · THE · CANADIAN · + · SOCIETY. · Collected·over·$6000·00

A portrait of Muggins, circa 1917, by Will Menelaws. Courtesy of
Christine O'Brien

Postcard of Muggins on a stand built for him by the Great War Veterans Association. Saanich Archives PR-149-2015-028-003

Postcard of Muggins with the Prince of Wales.
Saanich Archives PR-149-2015-028-006

Joseph Diggle as a prisoner of war. Courtesy of Margaret Broad

Naden Theatre, circa 1952. Built by hospital patients between 1915 and 1919, the Naden Theatre was razed in December 1964. This is where Muggins spent his final Christmas in December 1919.

Dr. Harry Keown, veterinarian of Muggins. By permission of Maureen McMichael Patterson, granddaughter of Harry Keown DVM

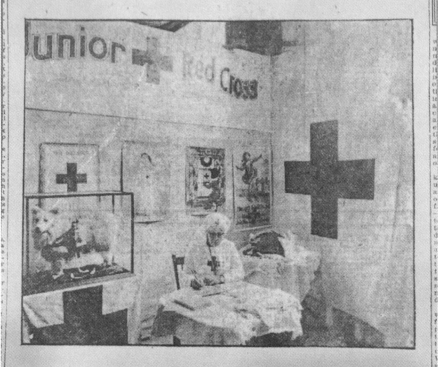

Junior Red Cross Exhibit at Willows Fair

Mrs. Harold Fleming, provincial organizer of the Junior Red Cross, opened her campaign in Victoria with a striking booth at the recent fair at the Willows. Specimens of the handiwork fashioned by junior members of other provinces were shown, while Muggins in life-like attitude added his mute appeal to the kiddies to join this splendid organization. Three thousand leaflets describing the aims and objects were distributed from this booth. Mrs. Fleming is working to secure the co-operation of the school authorities in this campaign, it having been proved in other countries that by organizing the school children greater results were accomplished.

A clipping from the *Daily Times*, October 9, 1920. This image of the preserved body of Muggins, displayed in a glass case, is one of the earliest to show how he was parleyed into donation collection and awareness raising not quite a year after his death. Saanich Archives

The collected medals awarded to Muggins. Saanich Archives

The author's partner, Rudi, with their dog, Freddie, on one of their Muggins-in-Victoria historical jaunts. Freddie stands where Muggins did in September 1919, when he was introduced to the Prince of Wales, at the base of the Queen Victoria memorial in Victoria's Inner Harbour.
Author's Collection

CHAPTER 5

The Price of Fame

ON THE DAY OF OUR ADVENTURE, FROM OUR vantage point at the Temple Building, Freddie and I looked across and down a few paces along Fort Street at another historic building with a link to Muggins.

Built as an investment property for Victoria businessman David Ker, the two-storey Edwardian structure was designed by noted architect Francis Rattenbury in 1909.[1]

At the time of writing, the building houses a Thai restaurant. But in early 1917, it served as a studio and display space for a Paris-trained Ontario artist named Mary Riter Hamilton; it may be from here that the artist first saw Muggins.

Perhaps Hamilton was standing at her door, or a window, or she glanced up when out of the corner of her eye she caught a glimpse of something white and fluffy moving fast along the sidewalk toward the Temple Building, then up its high flight of stairs. Hamilton may have watched for the phenomenon again, and finally confirmed that it was a dog and, after enquiries were made, that the dog was Muggins, Red Cross mascot and local fundraising celebrity. Hamilton, a deeply compassionate woman and a lover of dogs, was an artist who found inspiration in interpreting the mystery of life's moments, whether in the faces of politicians, the dynamic between mother and child, the ruined but not voiceless landscapes of battlefields, or in the eyes of Victoria's most beloved dog.

It is significant that when she would paint Muggins's portrait, he would be depicted in repose, much like the formerly hellish battlefields, lying quiet as birdsong trailed in clear air once heavy with smoke and reverberating to explosives.

Born in 1868 in rural Ontario, Mary Riter Hamilton had lost both her only child and her husband in swift succession. A young widow with aspirations to be an artist, she used the small inheritance from her husband to study in Berlin and Paris, much like Emily Carr, her junior by three years and with the same overwhelming need to pursue art education, used hers from her father to do the same.[2]

In Hamilton's day, as in Carr's, the proper sphere for a woman was, of course, the domestic one. No lady of quality worked or, heaven forbid, appeared in the newspaper except when she was born, when she married, and when she died. Like Carr, Hamilton was not above turning her gifts toward what we would now define as arts and crafts; though Carr is not known to have painted china (unlike other well-bred lady "artists" of her hometown, Victoria), Hamilton did, and she would later paint silk scarves to keep herself from starving in post-Great War France. Her greatest artistic and

Grant Hayter-Menzies

personal effort, and source of the most pain in the last part of her life, was her project to paint the battlefields on which Canadian soldiers had fought and died as they looked just after the end of the war, before nature's green reasserted itself.[3]

Hamilton's journey to France was sponsored by the Amputation Club of Victoria, an early version of Canada's War Amps, which raised funds to help war amputees obtain artificial limbs and other necessary supports. But that was where the funding ended, and Hamilton spent three years, often in starvation, living in huts and attics, creating some three hundred haunting landscapes, including that of Vimy Ridge. Unfortunately, due to a glut of war art after 1918, and a decreasing interest on the part of the press and public to cover any of the darker aspects of the war that had just ended, with tragedy for nations as for individuals, Hamilton ended up donating her paintings to the Public Archives of Canada. (One is reminded of Emily Carr's lack of success selling her paintings of Indigenous village life to the government of British Columbia, which—shockingly—professed to find them not "photographic" enough, a telling hint of how the bureaucracy of the day defined art.)[4]

This was a pattern that would persist throughout Hamilton's life; she was either struggling to earn enough money to eat and selling paintings for whatever she could get or, when briefly flush, generously giving them away to causes she believed in. Such would be the case with her portrait of Muggins, which dates from an earlier, happier part of her life as a popular and well-connected artist in Victoria.

Hamilton's first known appearance alongside Muggins in the Victoria press is in an article from

April 1917. While Muggins and Mrs. Duce's dog Peter collected for a tag day benefiting military hospitals, Hamilton donated her time writing "a number of lunch and tea cards for the canvassers, and to the daily press."[5] By that October, Hamilton had completed a portrait of Muggins which, true to form, she donated to the Canadian Red Cross to be raffled off.[6]

Though it reappears in the press for another few years—far from being raffled off, and far from being in the hands of the Canadian Red Cross, the portrait's next appearance after it was announced in 1917 is in January 1919, when it was reported to be sitting on an easel in the offices of the Development Association, an office that churned out enticements to visit and live in Victoria—the portrait has apparently been lost.[7] Dr. Sylvia Van Kirk searched for the portrait for years, but it is not listed in Hamilton's catalogue. Like the portrait of Muggins by Will Menelaws, which only recently resurfaced in England, it is certainly possible Hamilton's painting is hanging on a wall somewhere still, or stored away, and will also see the light of day eventually.

All we have to go by is this description of it in the *Daily Colonist* from October 1917. From this source we know the canvas measured 30" × 30" and depicted Muggins seated with the basket of flowers that stood on his collection table near the Empress Hotel:

> Strapped to his side is the familiar little white box [sic] with its Red Cross, and into which have been dropped from day to day the dimes, quarters, and occasional bills which have helped to total the sum he has to his credit. He is portrayed at his customary stand, corner

of Government and Bellevue [sic] Streets, where passers-by have found him faithfully at his post day after day. The background shows the long row of dark poplars nearby, a bit of sombre yet rich coloring which throws out into bold relief the alert figure and speaking eyes of the snow-white Spitz.[8]

Hamilton was a master in the use of lighting and shadow, in portraits as in her battlefield vignettes, and it may be imagined she made use of the same technique for Muggins, highlighting his white fur against dark branches, bright flowers beside him, and his "speaking eyes" gazing out from the canvas.

Why nothing more is heard about the proposed raffle we do not know. Perhaps it has something to do with an enormous disaster on Canadian soil less than two months later, not to be outdone until the nuclear bombs of Hiroshima and Nagasaki in the Second World War, for which Muggins would also collect relief funds—the December 6, 1917, munitions explosion in Halifax Harbour.

How, on a clear day, in a harbour with well understood rules dividing its entrance into two lanes, a ship with compartments and deck crowded with bomb-making materials could collide with another, despite opportunities to avoid doing so, remains something of a mystery. The *Mont-Blanc* was an aging vessel from France that had been loaded up—indeed, was overloaded—with munitions supplies and was preparing to head back across the Atlantic, where the Allies would make use of its cargo for bombs and guns. The *Imo*, a Norwegian ship, was on its way into Halifax Harbour, after waiting the night outside as anti-submarine nets had been strung across the harbour's entrance. Several small but ultimately enormous distractions—an American ship exiting the harbour in the wrong lane, a tugboat—led to the *Mont-Blanc* and *Imo* heading straight for each other.

Under ordinary circumstances the *Mont-Blanc* should have borne a sign on its sides indicating its dangerous cargo, but nobody wanted to take a chance of a German submarine seeing this and firing at the ship. And under any circumstances, the men in charge of such a vessel might be expected to go overboard, as it were, with extra precautions. They didn't, and the judgment or lack thereof of the Norwegian crew is impossible to assess, as they all disappeared in what happened next. The ships rammed each other, and fire began on the benzene-soaked *Mont-Blanc*, which started drifting toward shore. Its crew disembarked in life boats, screaming in French at all the other crafts within hearing to get away as fast as possible. A crowd gathered on shore to watch the spectacle of the flaming ship slowly making its way toward the city. After the explosion, which for its time was the largest man-made detonation then known, pieces of the *Mont-Blanc* were found several kilometres away. Two square miles of Halifax were flattened; thousands of people were dead or injured.

A massive aid effort got under way, with doctors, nurses, and disaster aid personnel from Boston, Massachusetts, first to reach the devastated city. In thanks, a Christmas tree has been sent from Halifax (whose first recorded Christmas tree dated back to the 1840s) to the people of Boston each year. Support for the people of Halifax followed from across Canada.

In Victoria, the Local Council of Women collected over $2,000 for Halifax relief, and it was noted that a number of wounded soldiers at Esquimalt Military Hospital, "who have already contributed generously," gave "substantial assistance" as well. Even residents of the Aged Ladies' Home made a gift. And Muggins and Peter were both included: a subscriber donated cash in both their names. Muggins's ability to raise funds for more than straightforward war effort but also for a disaster like the Halifax Explosion gives a hint at his post-war fundraising, as well as an indication of how far his fame had spread outside the boundaries of British Columbia.[9]

In July 1917, not quite a year since Muggins's collecting work had begun, Ellen Le Garde (1857–1925), a resident of Providence, Rhode Island, where she served as director of physical education for the Providence school system, happened to meet Muggins at his stand near the Empress Hotel, and wrote a letter that helps describe the magic this little dog engendered among wounded soldiers and the general public. Writing to the editor of the *Providence Sunday Journal*, Miss Le Garde sketched the scene: "Under a canopy of white, decorated with English Jack, French tricolour and now our own Stars and Stripes, this Siberian Spitz, since August 16, 1916, up to today, July 23, 1917, has collected for the Red Cross $3,000. He is five years old [sic], pure white, very aristocratic in bearing and watches keenly all the incoming passengers from the Seattle and Vancouver boats, taking up his stand daily at 12, only relinquishing it when the 4:30 PM boat for Seattle goes out. He, too, visits the Alaska boats, all the Princess[es] and the outgoing vessels for China and Japan. When he begins to ask for the Red Cross one chokes up and in go the coins, often gold, so common in this British Northwest.

They rattle in the Red Cross box [sic], strapped on his back and he barks his gratitude." Miss Le Garde was present when a shipload of wounded men arrived in Victoria Harbour. "Such faces. Such eyes!" she recalled. "Such maimed and butchered bodies!" She noted how the crowd could barely cheer for them—though most tried—because of tears. She also noted something else. When the ambulances and other vehicles drove past with the wounded inside, Muggins "looks up and barks, as if to say, 'I'm doing my bit,' and certainly for a dog he has."[10]

Photo features like the one displayed in Portland, Oregon's *Sunday Journal* in September 1917, showing a fluffy Muggins sitting up in his familiar "begging" pose, his collection tins displayed along with a faint hint of a smile (from artful retouching by the newspaper's photographic department), framed by the stripes of a Union Jack, underscored his smallness, his sweetness, his apparent willingness to serve, and the notion that if an animal could raise funds for the war effort, everyone admiring him on the page could "do their bit" as much or more than he did.[11]

Muggins was introduced to the rest of the American east coast when he was featured in a photo spread in the *New York Times*, flanked by photos of stage stars of 1917–1918 and scenes from the battlefields of France, with the caption: "For Months He Has Stood Daily on the Walkway from the Steamer Docks to the Business Centre of Victoria, Barking At All Pedestrians and Rattling His Red Cross Box [sic] For Funds."[12]

A photo of Muggins, along with a brief article about his collecting work, was featured in October 1917 in *Our Dumb Animals*, magazine of the Massachusetts

Society for the Prevention of Cruelty to Animals, beside which is an article by *Buffalo Medical Journal* editor Dr. A.L. Benedict, which could almost be directed at dogs like Muggins. "While the intelligence of dogs is no more to be judged from tricks than is human intelligence to be gauged by memorizing recitations or by acting," he writes, "the capacity of a dog to perform unnatural and difficult tricks under intensive training brings up a point in considering how far his intelligence can be compared with that of human beings under existing circumstances. Mere difference in longevity gives the dog about one fifth of the time to acquire knowledge and wisdom, as compared to man." Dr. Benedict goes on to point out that "the factor of available time is important and we cannot expect that the dog will acquire more than a fifth of the general wisdom and experience of the human being." Had he known Muggins's story—how young he was, how utterly unprepared he was in his pampered beginnings for the work he was carrying out for the war effort, and how much he had learned in so short a time—Dr. Benedict might have had more to say about Muggins's unique example of intelligence having nothing to do with years—even more ironic, and poignant, when we consider how short his life was to be.[13]

Muggins would again appear in the pages of *Our Dumb Animals*, in consequence of having met the Rev. Francis H. Rowley, President of the American Humane Education Society of Boston, at his collection stand in the Inner Harbour. That Rev. Rowley, just off his boat and eager to see Victoria, would be moved to stop at Muggins's stand is no surprise. A devoutly religious man, Rev. Rowley was convinced (perhaps with some naïveté) that what appeared to be a lack of compassion for animals fated for the slaughterhouse was in fact a lack of factual information about what happened within the walls of these establishments. He used photographs of animals being slaughtered, some of them while still living—including a terrible image of a calf being cut up by two nonchalant slaughterhouse workers—to press home the inhumanity and the immorality of causing pain and suffering to a living being.

In his early sixties when he met Muggins along the sidewalk, with white hair and moustache and bright eyes, Rev. Rowley was drawn to the fact that the dog remained in situ, never trying to jump down from his perch and showing a keen eagerness to engage with each passerby. On this particular day, it seems Beatrice was standing with Muggins because when Rev. Rowley dropped coins into his collections box, it appeared there were not enough or any of his postcards to give him in return. Promising to send the postcards when they were available, Beatrice penned a letter from Muggins to Rev. Rowley, dated May 9, 1919, which was reproduced in the July 1919 edition of *Our Dumb Animals*. In the letter, Muggins apologizes for the tardiness of the enclosed picture postcards, and tells Rev. Rowley about the charities his donations go toward helping, including the support of two prisoners of war in Germany, aiding the Red Cross, and so on. He also mentions that he had been ill: "I was a casualty for several weeks, as a result of an attack of influenza, contracted while on duty."[14]

As a patient of veterinarian Dr. Harry Keown, Muggins could not have been in better hands. A native of Ontario, the bright-eyed and moustachioed Dr. Keown had compassion for animals even before he attended veterinary college: his family remembers how, as a young man, he filed a lawsuit against a family whose servant, having found Harry's wanderlust-prone horse in his master's garden, tied it with a chokehold loop, so when the animal tried to flee it strangled to death.[15]

Dr. Keown had a special vehicle he used, marked with a sign that read CANINE AMBULANCE, for when an ailing animal was too sick or too big to be brought to his clinic. The clinic was located at Pandora Avenue and Cook Street, its large plate glass front windows filled with canaries in cages (bred and sold by Mrs. Keown as a sideline to her husband's work). Until the end of his career, Dr. Keown remained that same fervently compassionate man that he had been as a boy. He related to a reporter in 1924 how a little boy once came to his clinic with his dog, who was injured. The dog had been hit by a car, the boy said, and his father wanted to put it down. The boy couldn't believe this was necessary and so absconded with the dog to Dr. Keown's, where he knew he and the dog would be taken seriously—and that is just what Dr. Keown did. He discovered the dog had only suffered irreparable damage to two toes and he told the boy that the toes had to be amputated, but the dog would have a normal life. After the operation and the dog was bandaged and had rested, Dr. Keown sent them both back home with a note to the father, the contents of which we can only guess at. Easy to believe this was the man who, when called in the middle of the night by a household in Qualicum Beach whose dog had suffered a gunshot, drove one hundred and sixty kilometres through the dark to try to save it.[16] "Dr. [G.H.] Keown performed three operations on my chest," runs the sprightly letter that Muggins "wrote" to Rev. Rowley of Boston, "and I am now better, but the soldiers said I was a 'blighty' case while bandaged."[17]

Unlike his "mate," Lulu, Muggins had more reserves of strength and, perhaps, better luck. But as time would tell, however, heroism, even for a dog like Muggins, would prove to have serious physical limitations.

Grant Hayter-Menzies

CHAPTER 6

Armistice

AS THE WAR PROGRESSED, AND NEWS OF HIS WORK
reached beyond downtown Victoria, Muggins continued
to be featured in the press. This popularity brought
with it much that would gladden Beatrice and Muggins's
supporters, along with much that would cause them
both concern and even fear.

The *Spokesman-Review* of Spokane, Washington, devoted
most of a page in November 1917 to both the "remarkable
women of Victoria—and also of a wonderful Spitz dog."
The column's author, attorney Samuel R. Stern, writes as
if he had personally met Muggins at the Harbour, which
he likely had. After pointing out that in 1856, Queen
Victoria had bestowed the Victoria Cross on the survivors
of the Crimean War, Stern implies it would not be out of
place to suggest that Queen Mary "might most appropri-
ately bestow upon the city of Victoria, British Columbia
a new decoration of which the Red Cross should be the
particular symbol," pointing out the total support for the
war effort, often in massive contrast to the city's relatively

small population, and the fact the women of the city and environs had taken the lead in most of those efforts. Stern also applauds the work of non-human patriots. One of these, a fox terrier belonging to an avid golfer in Oak Bay, rigorously collected golf balls and brought them to his master, who donated them to the Red Cross Superfluities Shop (what we now call a thrift store), where their sale brought in regular revenue. If only we knew the dog's name! And, of course, Stern then turns to a dog who did have a name everyone knew. "He is a Spitz, with beautiful fur of pure white, with appealing eyes and apparently a taking way in general," Stern adds, as he was known to have collected thousands of dollars, each donation solicited on the ships and sitting on his table near the Empress Hotel. Two photos of Muggins, one from the series of formal portraits used on his postcards, and another of him sitting on his collection stand keenly studying the crowds in the Harbour, were placed in the centre of the feature.[1]

Victoria was not to be Muggins's only sphere of activity or influence. January 1918 had been one of Vancouver's coldest months on record, at -8 Celsius, and it may be assumed that February was not much warmer. Still, Muggins, who had been entered in the register as a guest of the then-elegant Hotel Dunsmuir, was placed for a tag day at the Main Post Office at 701 West Hastings Street, a silvery granite Beaux Arts structure with cupola clock tower finished in 1910. An article from 1939, based on recollections of people who knew Muggins, states that "If the day was chilly he would snuggle into a bear-skin rug, money-box resting between his forepaws," so in any event he would have had some protection from the cold.[2]

Grant Hayter-Menzies

Muggins was, according to the *Vancouver Daily News*, "much admired by all who saw him." Beatrice brought him back again in August, in time for what the *Vancouver Daily News* described as the anniversary of his collecting campaign. "On August 2, 1916," ran the report, "Muggins set out to raise the sum of $10,000 for various war charities, within the space of two years"—the first time in Muggins's public record in the press that we hear he was in fact working toward a set goal (which he was to exceed by more than half). "He goes about his work as though he really understood what he was doing it for," noted the columnist. It was while standing at his post outside the Main Post Office that Muggins was greeted by an Asian gentleman who had just come off one of the Pacific liners. Having heard that Muggins was in Vancouver, the man rushed to West Hastings Street to find him, and with great pleasure put a donation in his harness tins, just as he had first done on the same day in Victoria two years earlier.[3]

It is possible that this trip to Vancouver was combined with another Muggins took to Seattle that same month. He had been asked to the American city to help raise funds for the American Red Cross, as guest of the American military. Muggins, Beatrice, and Mrs. J.H. Holden, president of Victoria's French Red Cross, accompanied Muggins to Seattle on February 16, 1918.[4]

They seem to have first travelled to Camp Lewis, then brand new, as it had been laid out only the previous year. Muggins was "treated splendidly" there by officers and men. He then was taken to Seattle, where a reception was held in a theatre and where Muggins collected for the American Red Cross "a considerable sum." For his trip home, Muggins sailed north to

Victoria on the Japanese liner *Kashima Maru* (built in 1913 and sunk during the Second World War), accompanied by American troops and volunteer nurses whose ultimate destination was Siberia. To commemorate Muggins's work on behalf of American forces, an officer bestowed on him a bar pin which effectively made Muggins an honourary first lieutenant, awarded for foreign service. (This pin was normally worn vertically on a cap.) This bar pin would be one of eight known medals awarded Muggins over the course of his three years of fundraising work for the war effort.[5]

According to Samuel Brown Kirkwood, after the award of this bar pin, Muggins wore the American flag alongside the Canadian, and in fact the pin was altered just for Muggins: a small American flag in enamel was soldered to one of the long sides, and a silver banner engraved with "Muggins" was suspended from the other.[6]

If Muggins's fame preceded him wherever war news and newspapers were available, his ability to have a genuine influence on the lives of individual soldiers, through his fundraising for charity, proved to have no limit, either. "Somehow word came through from a German prison camp that two of the soldiers confined there—one boy was from Ontario and the other from New York—were badly in need of certain articles," wrote Samuel Brown Kirkwood. "Muggins supplied these."[7]

The particulars were revealed in a *Daily Colonist* piece from August 1919. The men referred to were Private Albert Crozier of the 19th Battalion (the "boy from Ontario") and Private Joseph Diggle of the 20th Battalion (who was not from New York but from Lancashire, thence to New York). Both were

Grant Hayter-Menzies

imprisoned at Dryotz, located not far from Berlin. Diggle, born in 1893, was five feet, eight inches tall, with black hair and blue eyes, and was living in Canada at the time of his attestation to serve in the Canadian Over-Seas Expeditionary Force; he gave his mother in Lancashire as his next of kin and his trade as farming.[8]

Crozier, from Leamington, Ontario, was also born in 1893; his trade was labourer. He had served in the First Hussars in Leamington. His mother, too, was his next of kin.[9] Why these two were in especial need is clear from the letter Diggle would write to Muggins, thanking him for the food packages sent to him, which arrived with a postcard of the dog tucked in.

Diggle, who later settled in Alberta, where he had a large family of children, grandchildren, and great-grandchildren scattered across the globe, sent Muggins this letter, which was printed in full in the August 24, 1919, edition of the *Daily Colonist*, by which time Private Diggle was released and in recovery:

> Dear Muggins,
>
> Your letter, dated July 31, has been forwarded to me. Well Old Timer, let me thank you for the grub you sent us to Germany. If it had not been for you and your pals, we would have been 'pushing up daisies' by now. Yes, Sir, between the two of us things weren't downright merry. We got so darn thin we had to stand up twice to make a shadow. We even reached the stage where a fellow wishes he had not done a few of the things he had and had done a few of the things he hadn't. That's Irish, but you'll know what I mean.

And then came Spring, and hand in hand my thread-bare patience apieces tore—Spring in the shape of a cardboard box with a little red cross. I'll never forget when the first one arrived. I was 'in dock' at the time, having my ankle operated on. Didn't we paste that tin of 'bully.' It was great, and the tea tasted like nectar of the gods. I've never tasted nectar, myself, but I know, darn well, it couldn't be equal to that tea. Well, after that 'tuck-in,' I felt as though I owned half Europe and had a mortgage on the other half.

Then the parcels began to come through regularly. There was a Russian prisoner, who used to do my washing occasionally in return for a bit of feed. The poor chap had been knocked about a bit and 'a shingle had worked loose.' The result was that he thought he was the King of Poland. He would come around and say:

"Englander, bread."

"Yes, your majesty."

An exchange of salutes with faces sober as judges.

"Have a drop of [chai], Russky?"

He would finish the tea and then wash up. I am not in the habit of associating with royal families. With the exception of King Edward and the King of Denmark, Russky was the only one I ever talked to. The others were so blamed busy they wouldn't even come to me for a drink.

Well, Old Timer, it's turned midnight, so I'll 'hit the hay'; but if we ever bump into each other, we'll be more sociable than the real kings were. We'll have a drink, too, even if it has to be 'two per cent.' So cheerio, Muggins, and thanks for the photo.

Yours sincerely, Joe Diggle[10]

Almost as significant to public interest as his fundraising was the announcement that Muggins had fathered a son. Called Vimy Ridge—Vimy for short—and born sometime in May 1917,[11] the pup's mother may have been Beatrice's other Spitz, Lulu, though this is not clear in view of a report that Lulu had "caught a cold" during one of the early funding drives with Muggins, which ended with pneumonia and death.[12]

In April 1917, the Canadian Corps captured Vimy Ridge, a valuable German-occupied escarpment. The Corps gained the high ground at enormous cost, but the taking of Vimy Ridge was to stand as not only a needed military victory for the Allies but as a coming-of-age rite for Canada as a nation. For the first time on the world stage, Canada proved what it could endure, and of what it was made. This battle was very much on everyone's mind that spring in Victoria, and clearly influenced the choice of name for Muggins's pup. During a concert evening at the Empress Hotel benefiting the Red Cross, raffle tickets were sold for the chance to own Vimy; the draw took place "in the presence of a number of excited youngsters and grown ups" at the Temple Building, where the holder of Ticket 242 (not identified in press coverage) "is now the happy possessor of 'Vimy Ridge,' the cunning little pup of Mrs. Woodward's famous dog 'Muggins.'"[13]

By the following winter, Vimy was said to be almost ready to go out collecting like his father, on behalf of returned soldiers, but given his age "the officers of the [Flower] Guild will be very glad to get the names of young ladies willing to undertake the role of chaperone for the pup."[14]

It's not known what happened to Vimy, but we do know that his splashy raffling in June 1917 led some local dog breeders to attempt to capitalize on his and Muggins's fame. Advertisements for "thoroughbred Pomeranians" sometimes included the eye-catching aside that the dogs were "like Muggins" (one of these advertisements was printed just above that of Emily Carr, offering bobtail sheepdogs for sale from her Simcoe Street apartment house to augment her paltry income as landlady, her fame as artist and writer many years in the future).[15]

That Muggins's puppies were considered premium stock can be deduced from a terse notice Beatrice placed in the pages of the *Daily Colonist*. "Mrs. Woodward, owner of Muggins, is annoyed at the announcement that reputed puppies of her famous Spitz, 'Muggins,' are being sold in the city. She wishes emphatically to state that no puppies of Muggins have been offered for sale in the city for the last 18 months with the exception of two that were sold at the Killarney stall this week"—perhaps the last of Lulu's litter. Beatrice's annoyance suggests this was far from the first time she had had to deal with opportunists trying to cash in on Muggins's name and fame.[16]

Unfortunately, for some people, Muggins represented a value that had nothing to do with his fundraising for the war effort.

The first week of July 1917, at around noon, two young boys were walking down a sidewalk in downtown Victoria, and approaching from another direction was Beatrice with Muggins, who was heading down to the Harbour to take up his position on his collection table in front of the Empress Hotel. We have to assume, based on what happened next, that Beatrice did not always have Muggins on a leash. In fact, though there was, and is, a city bylaw pertaining to this (with which Muggins, Beatrice, and several concerned citizens were to collide in future), perhaps Beatrice was of a mind that having been given freedom of the city to do his collection work on his own, which of necessity meant the dog could not be leashed at all as he went from the docks to Red Cross HQ and back, there was no need to use one in most instances.

So her shock may be imagined when she reached the location of the old Victoria fire hall (at 626 Cormorant Street, near City Hall), turned around, and realized Muggins had gone missing. The two boys did see what had happened: a car had stopped, a man had grabbed Muggins, and drove away with him. Frantic, Beatrice called the police, and a search was put out. Hours passed. At 5:30 PM, Muggins was found standing in the same place where he had been taken from. "The news was conveyed to Mrs. Woodward, who rushed to the spot to claim 'the prodigal.'" It was noted that Muggins was not wearing his donation boxes which would, in any case, not have been filled at that time of day. It is not impossible, however, that the thief believed he might be able to gain a ransom if he waited long enough, and when several hours passed and a ransom notice was not posted, decided it was not worth his while.[17]

Almost two years later, Muggins was stolen again.

This time, he was seated on his stand, finishing his afternoon's collecting at the dock, his boxes full. The woman (unnamed) who was looking after him in Beatrice's absence had to leave for a few minutes, and on her return Muggins (and presumably his donation boxes) were gone.

Beatrice contacted the police, claiming that this must be a case of theft rather than Muggins having run off, as he would never leave the stand on his own, a trait noted by several observers over the years of his public appearances. Soon the entire Red Cross was on the lookout for him, and police were covering the parks and beaches. The news brief describing the kidnapping indicates Muggins had still not been located by 9 PM. How, when, where he was recovered remain a mystery.[18]

These thefts were upsetting to everyone, particularly as their perpetrators were never caught and the fact that Muggins had been stolen twice meant it was even more likely it would happen again.

Neither of the thefts, however, made quite the explosive scene, including a face-off between citizens and local government, as the events of April 30, 1919.

The Empress Hotel we see today (in 2021) is not the building that Francis Rattenbury originally designed. Changes had to be made to the structure to increase the number of rooms and allow for growth. The familiar wing on the Humboldt Street side of the property was not yet in situ in spring 1919, and what was there was a long stretch of carefully clipped lawn. Beatrice later reported that she and Muggins were together on the grass, and as she removed his collection boxes—it was the end of his shift—she noticed a man looking at Muggins from across the street. Muggins was not leashed, but then, when he was working he did not wear one, and as we have seen, he likely wasn't put on one at all times. In what seemed to Beatrice a few moments, the man, who it turned out was the city pound keeper, Mr. J. Pitman, crossed over, picked Muggins up by the scruff of his neck, and crossed back to his van.[19]

Beatrice later said she was "much surprised," especially as Muggins was not on a public street but on the property of the hotel, where he was wholly permitted with or without a leash. Muggins was crying out from fear as well as from the fact he had just been operated on for a recurring abscess on his chest by his vet Dr. Harry Keown, and the wound had not completely healed. Beatrice followed them to the van, protesting and demanding that Muggins be returned to her. Passersby began to gather and they, too, circled the pound keeper, who, ignoring them, put Muggins in the back.[20]

The commotion soon caught the attention of others. One of these was Captain George McGregor. Born in Aberdeen, Scotland, in 1863, Captain McGregor was not quite fifty-six years old when he glanced out the window of his office in the Belmont Building and saw a ruckus taking place in the street below. McGregor was a man of purpose, talent, and initiative—his obituary, published in 1947, is mostly a lengthy list of the many worthy organizations and causes he aided throughout the course of his long and busy life in Canada.[21]

McGregor's office was close to the harbour because he had founded, in 1912, the Victoria Tugboat Company (his seven tugboats are listed, like children, by name on his bronze plaque at Belleville and Government Streets, incidentally across from where Muggins's donation stand normally stood). Whether by stairs or elevator, Captain McGregor was soon on the scene and trying to take charge. Knowing the law, he offered to pay charges for Muggins, but the pound keeper strangely refused. This raised the temperature as well as the number of onlookers and shouting voices to a fever pitch. Beatrice ran to her car and drove to Red Cross HQ to beg for help.

One of the onlookers hurried to a telephone and, managing to catch the mayor himself, told him the situation and that money had been offered to redeem Muggins. The mayor simply repeated what Captain McGregor had told the pound keeper when he offered to pay all charges. "You do know that this is Muggins in your wagon?" the pound keeper was told. Neither this nor the mayor's rather lukewarm contribution, nor anything else, made a difference. As if on cue, returned war veterans happened upon the crowd; shouldering their way to the van, they made threats if the man didn't let Muggins go. This in turn attracted the attention of a pair of police officers. One of them talked to the pound keeper, who was urged to use his common sense and let the dog go. This he agreed to do, but only if Beatrice was there to receive Muggins, which meant there was likely a wait until she returned from Red Cross HQ, parked her car, and made her way back through the crowd. "It seems that the reason for Muggins being arrested," reported the *Daily Colonist*, "was the fact that he was not on leash as required by law. Why Muggins, slow, dignified Muggins, should have been picked as the victim is hardly known. Some say he was the only dog that wouldn't run away."[22]

Grant Hayter-Menzies

A returned soldier named McKenzie put forward a resolution to Victoria city council the next day to discuss the actions of the pound keeper, and letters streamed in to newspaper editors and councillors alike.

A Muggins admirer named J.A. Shanks wrote a lengthy defence, which was published the day after the incident. "With reference to our old friend Muggins," he said, "who has done so much towards making the world safe for Democracy, I am surprised and provoked that his liberty has been assailed." Shanks outlined Muggins's work in downtown Victoria and elsewhere and his growing fame in and beyond Canada: "He is better known and more beloved than half the generals in the army." He also shared his low opinion of the city's leash law, and described the dangerous conditions in the city's pound which would have been Muggins's fate had the pound keeper not been stopped. "What we do need," he wrote in summation, "is one city father who will not be swayed by every absurd statement he hears about dogs, but will investigate and give the dog's side of the question decent consideration." While nobody sensible (though plenty who are not) would want to dismantle a law that keeps dogs safe on city streets, Shanks's critique of plodding, inflexible municipal bureaucracy is one that has a familiar ring to many of us today.[23]

I've studied a great deal about the Great War; it appears as a supporting character in most of my published work.

Like other writers who must deal not just with how wars happen, and how they are fought, and how they resolve (though the Great War, by any definition, was not resolved in 1918), I have never felt that I've plumbed the full depth of the experience. Nobody can.

What I know of what the Great War was like on the ground I learned from talking with my Scottish grandfather, John Menzies, who served with the Black Watch and Gordon Highlanders in France. Through his memories, I came to know the bravura of an underage (though six foot tall) boy who tried to join up in Aberdeen, was found out, and sent home, though not without a medal for trying; I learned of what it was like when he was old enough to join and took part in training, being shipped to France, and the hell of war his wide blue eyes encountered there. I saw the scars on his arm from the time a mortar shell exploded close by, burying him alive, and how, had a mate not seen his bloodied arm sticking out of the earth and dug him out, I might not be sitting here recalling the story today. And I can never forget his recollection of the Gurkha soldier. This man was taunted all day by a German prisoner of war, who dared him to show his *kukri*, or small sword, "because then you'll have to kill me, ha ha!" Likely to the German's surprise, the Gurkha soldier had had enough, and though the German POW was bound and essentially helpless (but for his foolish tongue), he was stabbed and killed on the spot. And I listened with awe as my grandfather reached back to faint but firm memories of the occasional truces along the front. He loathed the French, he admitted to me, and couldn't help but find much to admire in German organization, though no troops earned his reverence like the Gurkhas. "They were supermen, son!" he would say, eyes dazzled by the far-off memories, as if he'd had to squint in the light of bravery as bright as the sun.

The front page of the *Daily Colonist* in Victoria for November 11, 1918, gave a snapshot of virtually everything of critical importance that was happening at the moment the armistice was declared. It's a case of picking a crisis among a crowd of so many. Revolution broke out in Germany. The German Kaiser fled to Holland. French villages were freed of German occupation. Ominously, as events a little over ten years in the future would bear out, newspaper headlines—ARMISTICE TERMS MORE STRINGENT THAN FORECASTED— gave a hint of the demands that would be made on a beaten and broken Germany at Versailles, laying a powder trail to yet another world war.

A full-page editorial on the cover of the November 12 *Daily Colonist* makes for interesting reading, not least because it outlines the tasks that still remained now that the war was finally over:

> Show your thankful appreciation of the noble work that has been done by Canada's sons, in keeping you in business, your country intact and undisturbed. Your home and all you possess is still yours—your future has been assured and secured—your prospects are brighter than your fondest hope could dream of. Is it not your duty to think of the gallant lads, now resting in Flanders Fields, who will not return? Seriously consider the debt you owe these dear departed ones, who fell unflinchingly fighting for you and yours. These noble fellows will not respond to their names and numbers when demobilization takes place. They have died to save you from the iron grip of the enemy. Peace brings rejoicing—but sorrow is brought in its wake—and more than ever the loss of a father, a son, or a brother encircles the happy,

> unbroken home of four years ago. Peace is not all. The thinned lines must be brought home; they must be cared for and nursed back into civil life; their former occupations may not appeal to them, and even if they do feel inclined to carry on as before the war, we must not expect them to proceed to their various posts immediately upon their return.[24]

Peace is not all. For Muggins and for everyone who had been labouring to aid Canada's war effort over the past four years, those four words were never truer than on Armistice Day; and much of the work was now only to begin, even as the men who returned from battle would need help restoring normalcy to their lives.

First, though, there would be celebration that at least the most dangerous part of the battle was over.

The morning of November 12, anyone who was still asleep would have been awakened by sounds: the ringing of church bells across the city, blasts of ship horns from the Harbour. "It was the dawn of a day of tremendous significance for the world," the *Daily Colonist* opined. "It was 'The Day' par excellence." Newspaper carriers called out the glad tidings; citizens rushed to newspaper offices to make sure that what they were hearing was true. The mayor proclaimed a public holiday and a parade was organized for the afternoon, though it could be said innumerable parades were taking place all over town all day long, with decorated motorcars driven about filled with celebrants, horns tooting, whistles blowing, bells ringing. Confetti filled the air and the streets. The parade itself was the biggest in Victoria's living memory. Starting on Yates Street, it progressed from there to Douglas, Pandora, Government, View, Fort, Government, Menzies and Niagara, terminating at Beacon Hill Park near the memorial statue to poet Robert Burns. The weather, it was noted, was preternaturally cooperative. Dry skies and tearful eyes witnessed a procession that was headed by mounted police and the Fifth Regiment Band, "thousands of marching soldiers, sailors and civilians swung along amid cheering throngs."[25]

The band of the HMS *Lancaster*, whose sailors were particular friends of Muggins, was followed by military brass and the Women's Auxiliary of the Great War Veterans, for which Muggins had collected donations, themselves followed by over four hundred returned veterans who were given deafening cheers. Vehicles processed along bearing the Lieutenant Governor of British Columbia, Sir Frank Barnard and his wife, Lady Barnard, along with the French and Belgian consuls, the acting premier, the mayor of Victoria, and members of city council. Representatives from the Red Cross, the Blue Cross, the IODE, ship workers and firemen (from whose fire truck was suspended an effigy of Kaiser Wilhelm, looking worse for wear), and members of the Victory Loan organization.[26]

A photograph was taken of the parade along the Government Street route, showing the procession of Red Cross cars as they crossed Chatham Street (the Lim Dat Building, built in 1910 and still standing, can be seen, with Beatrice holding him steady, in the background). Toward the back, barely visible (and, had he not been white, totally invisible), Muggins can be seen sitting atop one of the ambulances his collecting had helped pay for. A banner hung alongside the vehicle announcing what to many in Victoria was common knowledge, but to others was thrilling and new information that Muggins had exceeded his $10,000 goal.[27]

There he sits, fixed in space and time, tongue out as he barks to cheering crowds. His work was not over, by any means, but what one little dog had achieved in the course of two years was and remains difficult to fully comprehend.

Born into a comfortable home where he had only to companion an elderly master, Muggins took to public life with ease, as if he'd been in the spotlight all his days. He'd learned specific skills in order to navigate that life, and while these were marvelled over by locals and visitors alike, they were really all based in one powerful need: to make Beatrice, and everyone with whom he was in contact, happy.

This he did, in material as well as intangible ways, by raising funds to support on-the-ground work on behalf of orphaned children, wounded soldiers and prisoners of war, nurses and doctors, and, as is too seldom pointed out, the animals conscripted into a war no animal ever caused.

It must have seemed to many in Victoria and those around the world who remembered and looked for Muggins on the Victoria docks that the little dog who "did his bit" would be around forever. The photos of him with soldiers and sailors, nurses and generals and politicians certainly support that impression. But on Armistice Day 1918, he would have only a little over a year left to live.

Which is why, impressive as all the events of his life are to us today, that last year enshrines Muggins as an indelible part of Great War history of his own time, whether or not he is as widely remembered as he deserves.

CHAPTER 7

Peace and the Prince

OVER THE COURSE OF 1919, THE POST-WAR POPU-lation assessed wounds physical, emotional, financial, political. They dealt with those wounds they could face full on, while others were left untreated, sometimes never to heal—and some of those festering wounds would inflame a second global conflict two decades later.

Soldiers who survived the Great War swung between euphoria to be alive and despair that friends or family were not.

Men returned home without faces, or arms, or legs, avoided by some, pitied by others, understood by few; some returned home different people from when they'd departed, unable to fulfill the roles they had played in peacetime, while others were able to push against their trauma enough to make a new life in what felt a different world.

Husbands and wives parted, or found new bonds in the babies that boomed from the post-war period.

Men like my grandfather, lucky survivors of the Western Front, returned to Britain long enough to toss a coin and head for greener fields abroad—in his case, Canada won out over Australia—to take the life that had been spared and do something with it to justify that good fortune.

People like my German cousins wrote letters to my grandmother, living in her father's comfortable house in Los Angeles, about how ruined the German economy was; how billions of marks, carried to the high street in a wheelbarrow, were needed to buy one loaf of bread. One reads the despair, confusion, and anger between the lines—which increased after the Treaty of Versailles, located with bitter irony on the spot where modern Germany had had its brief birth in 1871—exacted from Germany its very marrow, along with its bones. Punishment, most would agree, was deserved—but punishment that was politically wise, this was not.

Many who had fought on the battlefields of Europe and the eastern Mediterranean had to deal with their own personal Treaties of Versailles. Returning to life as it was normally lived was not possible, but return they must, and too often in order to do so they made a pact with life: give me back my family, and job, and the quotidian comforts of ordinary living, and I will not reveal my pain. Often this worked out just fine, but more often it did not. Which is why it mattered how these men—particularly the wounded, their survival mapped out in terms of learning to write right-handed or left-handed, to see out of one eye, or to navigate with none; donning a mask, or undergoing lengthy, agonizing, and not always successful plastic surgery, or making do with lungs shredded by gas—were received on their return home.

Wounded men had been brought to Victoria's convalescent hospitals since the war began. Now those who came at least knew they would not be returned to the front once they were better. But living in a hospital ward, often far from their home of origin, some with injuries that would take all their plans off course and, in some cases, take them out of the race entirely, was not entirely restful. They needed not just hospital beds and nursing and rest and to be fattened up or left to soak up the sun. They needed card games, and billiards, and music and books, and to enjoy all these pastimes together in something that was not a filthy dugout with a threat of death hanging over their heads as inexorable as gun smoke and mustard gas.

Even as he had done while they were fighting at the front, raising funds for bandages and socks and food and medicines, Muggins would serve his soldiers' needs for all they required in uneasy, troubled convalescence. He would do so with all the tangibles that were needed, and he would do so with the intangible therapeutic gift that was his simple presence at the hospital and military headquarters, where men were recovering as doctors and nurses looked after them.

Muggins's new year of 1919 did not start out much better than it did for countless numbers of wounded soldiers, not to mention the enormous swathes of the population around the globe sickened by the misnamed Spanish flu.

At the end of February 1919, passengers aboard the *Katori Maru* came down the gangplank to find a number of women selling postcards on behalf of the Red Cross. One passenger was standing quite still, as if looking for someone. A volunteer offered him postcards of Victoria in exchange for a donation, and he said, "I'm saving my money for the dog." It transpired he had been a frequent visitor to Victoria and had always sought out, or been sought out by, Muggins, and made a donation via his collection tins. He explained that on this sailing, he had told all the other passengers who did not already know about Muggins, the dog who had raised over $10,000, that they were in for a treat, and now he wasn't here, and he was upset. "This passenger had a gold half sovereign ready for those boxes, and where was the dog?"[1]

It turned out Muggins had been ill for two weeks. This was said to be due to influenza and to an abscess that had formed on his chest (mentioned earlier). From this remove, we simply do not know what was wrong with Muggins, only that both these conditions would be cited as serious enough to merit minor surgery and staying at home for fourteen days, an eternity for such an active dog. Beatrice's other Spitz, Lulu, was said to have died of a flu or cold caught while out canvassing for donations; perhaps she did not want to take any chances with Lulu's mate.

Possibly, both Spitzes had a genetic predisposition for pulmonary problems. This could also be simple coincidence, though this was not to be the only time Muggins suffered from lung infections. But the abscess on his chest suggests something else entirely. Could it be that all his running across town and up and down gangplanks and stairs, with heavy panniers full of coins on either side of his harness, had rubbed a spot on his chest that then became infected? "If no more abscesses form the celebrated canine will pull through all right," reported the *Daily Colonist*. This was why Beatrice herself went aboard ships in Muggins's place to sell postcards, knowing that everyone who made a donation would pester her about where the wonderful dog was, and telling her they were only doing it for him and would be looking for him in person soon.[2]

By early March, Muggins was still not well enough to work, but it was announced that the focus of his fundraising was to make a rather wide shift in focus. Aside from his work for the Great War Veterans Association, of which there would be more anon and would continue until his death, Muggins had been conscripted into service to an entity called the Development Association.

Formed to do pretty much that—foster development—the Association was in the public eye as far back as 1916. In a *Daily Colonist* piece titled "Making Victoria Known," the Association's goals were plainly stated: to provide publicity flogging Victoria's virtues in order to attract individuals and their money from elsewhere in Canada, specifically from the cold and snowy prairies, to the city where roses bloomed in winter and palm trees waved over the harbour year round.[3]

Two years later, in a piece titled "Prairie People Are Now Coming to the City," men visiting from the central provinces were described as wandering into the Association's office, having been directed there for more information about Victoria. The office was run by a Miss Taylor, who was accompanied by her pet Japanese spaniel. "That's the second kind of a dog that we have seen since we landed here that we have never seen before," one of the men said, with what the article seems to invite the reader to imagine are wide eyes, a hat pushed back from a sunburnt farmer's forehead, and some straw between his teeth. "It turned out the other animal of distinction was Muggins."[4]

If it seems a bit of a course change for Muggins to go from offering postcards of himself in exchange for donations to wartime charities, to carrying postcards featuring the Parliament Buildings, Empress Hotel, and various tourist sites around the city aboard the ships putting into Victoria Harbour, it's possible the Association was able to convince Beatrice to put him to this duty for the precise reason that in a post-war world, rebuilding and repopulating are part of pulling economies and societies back together—though no one would claim that selling houses in Victoria or encouraging tourists to visit in droves would ever replace what the Great War had taken from the city, province, nation, or world.

Still, a decade of conspicuous consumption lay ahead, alongside joblessness for veterans, untreated trauma from the horrors of war, and prohibition, all to be jumbled together into what would be speciously dubbed the Roaring Twenties. Meantime, business was business. "The Development Association have ordered one thousand [new brochures with Victoria views] for the famous [Muggins] in order to spread the news of the beauty of this city," ran a report from early March 1919. "Those which Muggins will dispense will have the Development Association's name on them." This would happen, the article runs on brightly, "when Muggins recovers sufficiently to get on the money collecting work again at the boats."[5]

As if to recast the dog as mascot of city development and commerce, the Development Association somehow obtained the Mary Riter Hamilton portrait of Muggins, which "will adorn the office of the Association . . . upon a hand-carved easel."[6]

If the Development Association was rather wide of Muggins's traditional area of work, it was still only to be a small part of it. The Red Cross was to continue to benefit as before, along with the Great War Veterans Association, which later became the Legion system. Where the latter was concerned, plans were being laid long before the war was close to being over. In February 1918, the *Cowichan Leader* in Duncan printed a front-page feature covering a public meeting that gave all available information about the concept and structure of the Association. Returned veterans were among the audience, along with the members of governance for the Association. "The G.W.V.A.," runs the article, "aimed to hand on the esprit de corps and the glorious traditions of the Canadian army to future generations." Under no condition, stated the local official who stood in for the absent mayor, would there be a repeat of the Boer War, when veterans returned to their homes and asked for jobs, only to be told no.[7]

Association representatives appealed to all those who had served in the war, as much as those who had not, and addressed concerns obviously voiced loudly enough in the community. Would the GWVA be a make-work organization which secured jobs for returned vets just to keep them busy? What had fighting in this bloody conflict done to the men who fought, and how had the carnage reshaped their characters? Could they be trusted? When given jobs, could they handle the work-load and responsibilities as required? Far from being shirkers, it was said, "men who had fought for their own country placed a higher value on it than those who had not . . . They were ready to come back and work for it as they had fought for it." The GWVA's objective embraced more than returning veterans' needs. It also aimed to provide "service to those who had suffered, to care for the maimed, widows, and orphans, watch their interests and help them in every possible way," including dependants from abroad, a sticky issue with taxpayers who feared high taxes would be legislated to support them.[8]

One of the causes the GWVA worked toward was a "new house" fund, which was to be spent on acquiring Patricia Hall, a two-storey brick building next to the Montrose Apartments on View and Blanshard Streets, for a total of $40,000.[9]

It was for this cause that Muggins collected donations. This time, a special stand was built for him, draped in bunting and flowers, with his name literally in lights on a sign overhead, along with another one below where he sat outlining his collection total to date. His stand was situated roughly where the British Columbia Legislature Cenotaph, unveiled in 1925, stands today on the Parliament Building grounds.

Many donations were also directed through Muggins to benefit the Esquimalt Convalescent Hospital, which, besides treating the men for their injuries, was serving them as a home away from home and sometimes as the only home some of them had.

A convalescent hospital had been in place at Esquimalt Naval Base since 1865; it was a royal naval base until 1905, when it was handed over to Canada. From 1915 until 1922, the hospital's chief aim was to care for soldiers suffering from shell-shock, wounds, and tuberculosis, and this was care that involved much more than medical attention. Healing interior wounds can take much longer than the healing of exterior damage. That esprit de corps promoted by the Great

War Veterans' Association was best developed when men could get together in group activities of a nature very different from those they had survived on the battle-field. In the battle for a return to normalcy, a game of cards or billiards or singing around a piano with fellow patients offered that equilibrium. These items were not easy to come by during the war or in the depressed economy that followed. So Muggins stepped in to make things right. A local news report from July 1919 spelled it out clearly:

> A dog's life is not so bad. Last night Muggins, famous Red Cross cash collector, went aboard the *Empress of Asia* at the Outer Docks and in addition to his usual rich haul from passengers on the liner he received four $100 bills in his boxes from Capt. Davison. Capt. Davison was given the money by a passenger on his last inward voyage. The man saw the dog outside the Empress [Hotel] and when he went back to the ship he gave the skipper the sum named . . . The money goes toward the furnishing of a billiard room at the Esquimalt Convalescent Hospital.[10]

On July 17, a hut like those known to soldiers from the front in everything but its interior was opened at the Convalescent Hospital, funded by the Victoria Red Cross and Muggins.

Red Cross officers, workers, returned soldiers, and family and friends were present for the reveal. Major-General Robert G.E. Leckie, a special friend of Muggins's who had posed with him for a photograph on the steps of the Bay Street Armoury, formally received ownership of what was described as a "cheerful walled-in pavilion with its comfortable furnishings, pretty chintz cushions, and dainty curtains." Fred Jones, head of the Victoria Red Cross, made remarks in which he pointed out that none of the monies collected by the Red Cross had been expended on salaries but only on supplies, and he gave special mention to Muggins, who sat watching everything with interest, by pointing to a Heintzman piano on the hut's small stage. Entirely through the dog's efforts, he said, was the piano purchased for the soldiers. Much to the delight of the men, Jones added that "rumor had it [Muggins] was already busy collecting toward a further billiard table."[11]

A few days after his appearance for the opening of the new pavilion at the Convalescent Hospital, Muggins was the centre of attention once again during the Peace Day Parade that enveloped Victoria in flowers and a sense of renewed hope in humanity's forward progress. Beginning in the early morning of July 19, "the spirit of rejoicing was in the air," reported the *Daily Colonist*, "rejoicing over probably the greatest single event in history—the signing of a definite peace treaty at the conclusion of the world's greatest war." [12] (Note the careful "probably": doubtless few newspaper editors or anyone else wanted to attempt to gainsay Fate after what the Great War had taught them.)

"Victoria was ablaze with color," the report continued. "Scarcely a building in the city but honored the occasion with flags, bunting and various patriotic emblems, while vehicles of all kinds, from the luxurious high-powered cars of millionaires to the jaunty little pony cart, displayed something in the way of decorations." Every building of note was decorated; one company had donated a large peace arch made of flowers.[13]

It was estimated that almost ten thousand people crowded into Beacon Hill Park, Victoria's pride and joy, which was the terminus for the parade and the location of remarks made for the occasion by dignitaries, including Victoria's mayor Robert J. Porter, Lieutenant-Governor Sir Francis Barnard, Major-General Robert Leckie, and the premier of British Columbia, John Oliver. (The latter three were admirers of Muggins and were photographed with him at various times during and after the war.) Muggins had been carried up to the park on the roof of a service ambulance, held in place there by Doris Baker, a niece of Beatrice's. Even in the crowded throng of floats that moved slowly up Government Street to the park, Muggins and Doris can easily be seen: the white dog beside the girl in white; Muggins with mouth open and barking to the crowds, Doris waving with a smile. A banner attached to the ambulance spelled out the words many had come to associate with Muggins: STILL DOING HIS BIT.[14]

In early November, the Empress Hotel was the setting for a twelve-hour-long event meant to "advertise" the J Chapter of the IODE, "and to reveal its enterprise" through a bazaar, fashion show, and musical entertainment, but it was in fact very much a showcase for Muggins. We don't know whether he was in the Empress ballroom the entire time—Muggins was a patient dog, and an obedient one, but there is only so much of a bazaar, fashion show, and musical entertainment that anyone, including a dog, can undertake. There was dancing to the strains of Professor Lou Turner's orchestra, and the whipping and whirling of gowns and trains during the waltz must have proved diverting for Muggins. There was singing, and "Mrs. Seldon [sic] Humphreys, attired in a most bewitching dress, sang 'Come on Papa,' which we are assured was 'one of the hits of the evening.'" Given that the song is about a sex worker called Sweet Marie who, after the Great War, drives around Paris picking up American doughboys, to whom she says, "Come on papa/ Hop in ze motor car/ Sit by mama/ And hold ze hand," there may have been a few Victoria dowagers present for whom "hit" had a very different connotation.[15]

Far from being a lady of adjustable morals, Mrs. Humphreys, wife of Major Arthur Selden Humphreys, had been born Kathleen Euphemia Dunsmuir and was daughter of James Dunsmuir, former premier of British Columbia and builder of Hatley Castle (now Royal Roads University), whose father was the Nanaimo and Victoria coal baron, Robert Dunsmuir. A woman of gifts and great *joie de vivre*, her life was not unique in being defined by war, but her willingness to face war down when it came again in 1939 would prove fatal.[16] Keeping up the merrymaking, Arthur Sinclair Gore, who had worked with architect Samuel Maclure (designer of his Rockland bungalow home) and manager of the Electric Blue Print & Map Co., sang a round of what was presumably "Princess Pat," the "repeat after me" song well known in the military and among the Girl Guides, with its comic nonsense lines echoed back to the singer by his audience:

> The Princess Pat
> Lived in a tree
> She sailed across
> The seven seas

Grant Hayter-Menzies

> She sailed across
> The Channel too
> And she took with her
> A rick-a-bamboo . . .[17]

"One very interesting episode," the report continues, "which was not included in the original programme was the presentation to 'Muggins' of three medals in recognition of the splendid work he has done collecting for various good causes since the war began." These were the Croix Rouge Française, a Great War Veterans Association (GWVA) badge, and YMCA badge. The French Red Cross medal, plain silver emblazoned with a vivid red enamel cross, was bestowed "in acknowledgement of the abundant help given by Muggins in collecting for the destitute children of France." As the medal was pinned onto Muggins's halter, the ballroom orchestra launched into the French national anthem, "La Marseillaise." The GWVA medal was accompanied by a letter which conveys a growing sense among the military at least that Muggins was close to or already in retirement, and deserving of same, from his frenetic fundraising activities: "We trust that most of your hard work is over and that you may continue to live a happy and faithful life with your mistress and master."[18]

In fact, Muggins would wear his medals, to which were added his Boys of Lancaster Navy badge and his American First Lieutenant's bar pin, not long before Christmas in a funding drive for undernourished Victoria children held outside Wilson's Drug Store. It was the first time he was seen in public sporting all his medals and, though no one could have guessed, the last.[19]

One of the tragedies of the life of Prince Edward, Duke of Windsor, formerly King Edward VIII, is that his affable human attributes tended to work as much against him as they did for him.

He was roué, humanitarian, playboy, populist, all at once. He could shift from affairs with married women to charming disaffected unemployed miners, with whose lives and experiences he had not the remotest atom in common yet whose allegiance he could summon with an open and authentically friendly smile and an honest question: What can I do for you?

David, as he was known to his family, had "the common touch." When he was once caught by a housemaid bringing his breakfast tray *in flagrante delicto* in bed with his married mistress Freda Dudley Ward, the prince later sought the maid out in a corridor and gave her a brooch, thanking her for a discretion that his gift implied he would prefer she maintained for the foreseeable future.[20]

Edward was a reluctant royal star who, as his biographer Philip Ziegler has written, brought such genuine sympathy to visits to military convalescent hospitals that he, like an actor who cannot pace himself but burns at constant high flame, was exhausted by the end of each day.[21]

Yet Edward amusedly and rather dismissively termed these outings, which mattered a great deal to his future subjects, "princing." And while this was a prince who could write to his parents, "I'm rubbing it in that although not actually a Canadian born I'm a Canadian in mind & spirit," Edward's way of "becoming"

Canadian was to purchase a ranch in Alberta that he was never to occupy. His notion of personal freedom was less tied to national character, more so to a personal inability to focus on responsibilities.[22] His father, King George V, had harsh words for him that, allowing for hyperbole, rang more true than not: "You dress like a cad. You act like a cad. You are a cad."[23]

Edward was better than that, by a small margin, but he was above all a man for whom principle would seem to matter no more than the royal restrictions he found so unbearable, yet whose one shred of principle stood its ground when he was asked to make what for a hereditary monarch is the ultimate painful choice: between the woman he loved—twice-divorced, scandal-tainted American Wallis Warfield Spencer Simpson—and the throne. It was a choice for which he would pay dearly, perhaps more than he estimated. The handsome prince with the winning ways and ideas for reform had had his kingdom in the palm of his hand, and for what some saw as romantic reasons and many saw as selfish reasons, he threw it away, ending up an ex-king and a sort of pseudo-royal whose visit with Adolf Hitler in 1937 is seen as extraordinarily bad judgment for one who once occupied the British throne. He and his wife, who was denied the style Her Royal Highness, adopted a very different style, that of café society habitués, and rumours abounded about the nature of their relationship, the Duchess of Windsor's moral character, and the sort of tabloid fodder that keeps papers in business.

That chapter of Edward's life was very much in the future, however. When he started his tour of Canada in August 1919, he was every bit the royal celebrity. He and his entourage swept across Canada from east to west. He addressed crowds, talked with everyone who wanted to speak with him, allowed himself to be taken into the company of veterans to talk about war days— "Put it right here, Ed. I shook hands with your grand-dad"[24]—and indeed he shook so many hands his right palm and arm became bruised and sore and required the use of his left, a circumstance which Queen Mary thought undignified.[25]

Regardless of these conditions, Edward continued to review troops, accept flowers and gifts, listen to speeches, and tried his best to conduct "princing" in a way bearable for him and worth experiencing by cheering Canadians. After all, as he candidly wrote in his memoir, "My private evaluation of my own worth had previously not been particularly high, but the Canadians in their kindly enthusiasm almost convinced me that they liked me for myself, an act of open-heartedness that did my ego no end of good."[26]

American photographer Tracy Mathewson (born circa 1875) was on hand in Victoria's Inner Harbour when the Prince of Wales's vessel, the *Princess Alice*, sailed in on September 23. Published in 1936, the year Edward VIII abdicated for the woman he loved, Mathewson's notes for the prince's visit were made from a privileged vantage point, as photographer appointed to accompany the royal tour.

After spending the night at the Empress Hotel, Mathewson says, Edward appeared in his uniform at the Parliament buildings on a clear, bright autumn morning. On the lawn in front, "veterans, naval training school cadets, Boy Scouts, Girl Guides and nursing sisters lined up to a great hollow square" surrounded on all sides by crowds of Victorians—estimated at around twenty thousand persons—all eager to catch a glimpse of the star heir to the throne. "Hundreds of school children were massed along the steps [of the formal entrance] leading up to the buildings," reported the *Province*, "cheering vociferously and waving Union Jacks and Canadian ensigns as His Royal Highness drove up."[27]

Standing on the steps, Edward, with the lieutenant-governor, premier, and their wives nearby, listened to a number of civic addresses. After inspecting the veterans and presenting military awards, the prince met with the children of soldiers killed in battle. He then proceeded down the walkway past the fountain to the site of the planned memorial statue to Queen Victoria. Children on either side scattered flowers in his path. "He walked straight to the monument," remembered Mathewson, "and placed a wreath at the base" of black granite stone. The prince ceremonially set the cornerstone and was given a silver trowel as souvenir, while another was sent to the safekeeping of the legislature archives. It was then, said Mathewson, "that Muggins was presented to the Prince." Instead of the Red Cross emblem, his collection boxes bore that of the Great War Veterans Association.[28]

> If you've never heard of "Muggins," you should have, because he is the most remarkable Spitz dog I have ever seen. The Prince took a liking to Muggins and stooped to pat his head. And Muggins "fell" for the Prince, because he licked his hand and looked at him with his understanding eyes as much as if to say: "You're a friend."[29]

With Muggins was Beatrice's niece Doris Baker, dressed like all the children that day in bright white lace and ribbons. With a curtsey, Doris presented Muggins's photograph to the prince, who said:

> You love Muggins, I love Muggins, Victoria and the whole Empire love Muggins. I shall treasure this picture of this grand dog and keep it among my souvenirs at home in London. Among the defenders of civilization may be reckoned some of the four-footed creatures. Thanks, Muggins, thanks again and again, for to you as well as other animal friends of man, is due a large portion of the Empire's success. Muggins, in the name of the Empire, I salute you.[30]

Many who read accounts of the prince's shooting habits, and those of British aristocrats in general, might not have believed it, but from childhood onward, Edward loved animals. As a boy, he had been pained at the sight of fish caught on hooks; and while his natural instincts toward animals had been brought more in line with his status over time—that of an aristocrat for whom hunting and shooting were as part of the fabric of everyday life as drinking tea—he continued all his life to love dogs. He and the duchess were to serve as "parents" of whole families of pugs at their Paris residence. So we may take his speech to Muggins with the sincerity with which he delivered it, and though the photograph Muggins gave Edward is nowhere to be found, it likely did grace the prince's—and then king's— study until choices he made in 1936 for the woman he loved scattered the nation's hopes and wishes for him as well as everything that was settled and secure about his life in the nation of his birth, where he was never to live again.[31]

As for Muggins, we cannot know what this brush with royalty meant to him. A photograph, later circulated in the form of postcards, was taken of the meeting. It doesn't capture the prince kneeling to Muggins, or Muggins licking his hand, but shows Doris Baker presenting the photograph of Muggins to Edward, with Premier Oliver and Lieutenant-General Barnard on hand to explain. Muggins has turned to look directly at the camera and appears to be panting in excitement; adding to this impression of stress is the lifting of one paw, often a signal that a dog is confused and is not certain what to do next. If the crowd was as large that day as estimated, it was still not much larger than what Muggins had faced from the tops of floats in the parades he had taken part in. I prefer to see this photograph as the moment before the prince knelt to greet the little dog personally, calming and reassuring him as he said, "In the name of the Empire, I salute you!" and receiving Muggins's pink tongue in return.

Nobody present could have guessed in their wildest dreams that this was the "sturdy little dog's" last turn in the sun.

CHAPTER 8

Last Christmas

THE WEEK OF CHRISTMAS 1919 WAS A BUSY ONE for Muggins.

On December 20, he and Beatrice were stationed at Wilson's Drug Store, their accustomed spot for so many tag days of the past three years. The IODE was holding a milk drive for undernourished schoolchildren, and with Muggins wearing all his medals thus far received, there was "unusual interest" in the fundraising drive, according to the *Daily Colonist*.[1] Perhaps post-war exhaustion, after the euphoria of the armistice and the visit of the Prince of Wales, proved a dampening influence: the IODE aimed for $1000, but made somewhat less ($860).[2] Was it perhaps time to follow the spirit of the letter Muggins received along with his GWVA badge— "We trust that most of your hard work is over and that you may continue to live a happy and faithful live with your mistress and master"—and give him a rest?[3]

Muggins had been busy at the docks all of December, collecting from passengers on the *Empress of Asia* and the

Makura Maru. Beatrice divided up his takings among charities with specific Christmas needs: the Rotary Club Christmas tree fund, including the IODE Christmas tree collection for orphans and widows, the Friendly Help Society, and the Salvation Army, among others. Curiously, at the end of the notice, which ran in the Christmas Eve edition, Beatrice extended thanks to all the officials and staff of liners, Canadian customs, Outer Wharf, and Canadian Pacific Railroad, "who have by their unfailing courtesy and kindness contributed so much to the success of Muggins's efforts." Was Beatrice beginning to think it was time for Muggins to retire?[4]

That evening, the windows of the red brick buildings of Esquimalt Convalescent Hospital were brilliant squares of light in the chill gloom.

The same IODE unit for which Muggins had raised funds on December 20 had organized a Christmas celebration for the patients. Starting at 5 PM, the men were treated to dinner in the hospital's dining hall, which the IODE ladies had decorated with "lavish profusion of fir boughs, holly, Christmas bells and other festive decorations." The men were seated at tables before a repast of Christmas delicacies, which many of those who had served in the trenches hardly remembered from before the war, and which many civilians in the post-war inflation period rarely saw, if ever, because few could afford them. A charming touch: "the hospital staff, including doctors, nurses and orderlies, acted as waiters performing nobly their self-appointed task."[5]

Dinner finished, everyone went out into the cold night to the Recreation Hut, a wood frame building that had just been constructed that year. "In one corner stood a huge Christmas tree, illuminated with vari-colored

lights, glittering ornaments and Christmassy packages."
Father Christmas was impersonated by a most revered
figure, Canon Joshua Hinchcliffe. Born in Bradford,
Yorkshire, in 1868, Rev. Hinchcliffe was a man of many
gifts: he was a reverend who could build his own church,
as he did in Red Deer, Alberta[6]; he served in the British
Columbia provincial cabinet as Minister of Education
and Minister of Lands; and during the Great War he
served as chaplain to the Canadian Expeditionary Force.
He even helped translate the Blackfoot Prayer Book in
1899.[7] Canon Hinchcliffe distributed the presents—
pipes, tobacco pouches, cigarettes, and playing cards to
the men. "His pertinent remarks anent the little idiosyn-
crasies of each recipient as he or she came up to receive
the gift, kept the assembly in a continual state of merri-
ment." The evening finished with a dance that went on
until after midnight.[8]

Muggins was also a guest, alongside Beatrice, with
the chairman of the Red Cross and several others either
involved in planning the evening, running it, or who
had been part of the fundraising machine during and
after the war. We don't know how long Beatrice stayed,
or how long Muggins spent sitting at her feet or sleep-
ing under her table. Given his fame among the men,
and the respect with which he was held, it is doubtful
Muggins was able to sit or rest much during the several
hours of that joyous occasion.

It was later written of that December week by Ann
deBertrand Lugrin, who knew Muggins well, that
he had "caught cold at Christmas time when he was
making his last collections for the Orphans' Christmas
Tree fund."[9] We now know that dogs cannot catch cold
from humans; though, during the COVID-19 pandemic

of 2020, the World Health Organization reported that some pets had apparently caught the virus from their human guardians, there was no immediate evidence that they could transmit the virus to humans themselves, or that the virus was as damaging to them as to humans.[10]

According to newspaper articles from the time of the so-called Spanish flu, some people were fitting masks to their pets' faces in an effort to protect them from the virus. I have not seen a photo of Muggins wearing a mask, nor any report connecting him in any way with the deadly flu that decimated the Victoria population after the Great War as it did so many communities around the world. Could he have picked up the virus from the public? It's possible, but also not as likely as that Muggins was simply exhausted by the busy season, his fourth year of full-time fundraising activity. His mate, Lulu, had died of pulmonary disease years before, allegedly in consequence of her donation collection work in downtown Victoria. If she and Muggins were related, as seems likely if both were from the same litter in Emmeline Hull's Calgary kennels, perhaps, as I have suggested, there was a genetic predisposition to lung ailments.

Regardless of genetics or the Spanish flu, it is possible Muggins was already ill when he was brought out to the convalescent hospital that evening. Was Beatrice unaware of this? Did she know, and was she giving Muggins what she feared was to be his last outing with the soldiers who loved him?

All we know is that Muggins died on January 14, 1920. His *Daily Colonist* obituary appeared in print the very next day: "It is with very genuine regret that citizens yesterday learned of the demise of Muggins, the wonderful dog which since the commencement of the war in 1914 [sic] became famous through the length and breadth of the Empire for his work in collecting for various patriotic funds."[11]

Using the several obituaries published across Canada and abroad, we can reconstruct, within reason, approximately what happened.

Shortly after the week of Christmas, Muggins was determined by his vet, Dr. Harry Keown, to have pneumonia. He had already had, as we have seen, a number of instances where chest infections had become serious enough to keep him home for weeks at a time. Dr. Keown treated him, but this was decades before antibiotics were prescribed for animals, and it is not clear what would have helped to fight the infection. If Muggins was already compromised due to exhaustion, as suggested by the obituaries, it's not clear what could have been done to stop the illness as it made inroads. Despite everything, Muggins got worse, but Dr. Keown continued the fight: he "did everything within his power to save the life of the renowned Spitz."[12]

Muggins suffered for a total of two weeks, in an era when most guardians would have had him euthanized when told there was no hope. That the Woodwards continued to hope is obvious.

But hope has it limits. On the night of January 14, Dr. Keown drove out to the Woodwards' Gorge Road house three times, called back by Beatrice as Muggins's breathing became more and more laboured. Dr. Keown, like most veterinarians—and like many who worked for animal shelters, which saw death as a release from the hell of life as a homeless stray—had a system in his clinic for euthanizing sick or badly injured animals not likely to recover. In fact, when he was interviewed years later, he showed to the reporter a kind of gas chamber that served this purpose. This form of inducing a "humane end" was viewed, through the lens of the time, as superior to chloroform, which was later replaced by sulphurous gas, and finally carbonic gas, with various other methods tried and abandoned due to observed suffering in the animal being exposed to it.[13]

None of the obituaries says so, but it is probable that on Dr. Keown's final visit that night, seeing the dog struggling, and the Woodwards' distress, the veterinarian convinced them to let him do the only humane thing possible. Some time after midnight, in the early hours of January 15, Dr. Keown eased Muggins into a peaceful death, probably with an overdose of sedative.[14]

All reports agree that Beatrice was devastated by Muggins's death. It cannot have helped her emotional state to read in one obituary after another, "it is not at all improbable that it was in connection with his final 'appeal' [outside Wilson's Drug Store in downtown Victoria before Christmas] that he caught the chill which resulted in his death"—indeed, perhaps this was by her own admission.[15] Nor can it have helped when rumour was spread that Muggins had died of tuberculosis, a cause of death sure to concern the many mothers whose children had petted and spent time alongside Muggins in his collecting work. But a post-mortem by Dr. Keown made it very clear, according to a terse newspaper report: "Dr. Keown stated that he was able to state authoritatively that the popular dog's death was due to pneumonia, as was first stated."[16]

Grant Hayter-Menzies

A local poet, Guy Manners, wrote a poem which was published in the *Daily Colonist* on January 15, 1920.

> Muggins: A Tribute
>
> Had I the gift to make you understand,
> The sort of hero that you were and are;
> 'Twould do me good to shake your blessed hand
> And whisper that your soul will journey far:
> Far unto a better world than this
> Where comrades wait you for the good you've done,
> And they'll be waiting, holding solemn tryst
> With Him whose throne reflects the radiant light of sun.
> Dumb though you were, you had an almost human soul;
> Had you been man you would have offered up your life
> Where bayonets flashed; you would have paid the toll
> And died to save the world from future strife.[17]

Perhaps most moving of all is the short note one Ella Hayward sent to the editor of the *Daily Colonist*. "The first thing when I got up this morning was that I saw little Muggins' picture. I thought Muggins had done another great deed. But when I read it, to my great disappointment I saw that poor little Muggins died . . . I have a dear little cat by the name of Muggins, and I only wish it was a little dog, and I would take dear little Muggins' place, as he will be missed by all the Victoria people."[18]

In March, a posthumous medal arrived in the Woodwards' postbox.

Of all the medals and badges Muggins received, this one most touches those who see it today; we can only imagine what its arrival did to Beatrice. The medal came from the Esquimalt Military Hospital. On its verso was engraved into the gold surface TO 'MUGGINS'—IN APPRECIATION OF HIS SERVICES.

On its face, in a scrolled circle flanked by oak leaves, was a bas relief figure of Muggins himself, his Red Cross collection boxes hanging from his harness, his face turned with his customary curiosity and determination toward the viewer. In military symbology, the oak leaf denotes "mentioned in dispatches" for acts of valour or other noteworthy actions. The leaves on Muggins's posthumous medal may have been part of a predetermined design, but they are appropriate for the little dog who, had newspaper accounts of his charitable works been military dispatches from battlefields, would have covered him in more golden leaves than all the oaks of Beacon Hill Park.

CHAPTER 9

Death and Life

ON ONE OF MY LAST DAYS IN LONDON, ENGLAND, IN October 2018, after a busy book launch followed by sightseeing, I had some free time, and I decided to use it to visit a museum dedicated to the memory of a woman who has been, since my childhood, a hero and an example to me of the best of being human and humane—Florence Nightingale.

Located at St. Thomas' Hospital in Lambeth, the Florence Nightingale Museum is a place like many dedicated to a single influential personage. Inside, past the gift shop (also always a part of such places), there are exhibits related to Nightingale's family and childhood— landed gentry, at whose country place the young Florence collected animals she had doctored when ill and country folks to whom she showed similar compassion—with the preponderance of space dedicated to her ground-breaking work as nurse during the Crimean War and the innovations she brought to nursing that helped shape the profession we know today.

A special exhibit was on that, in this centenary year of the end of the Great War, focused on nursing in the war and in the flu pandemic that followed it in 1919. Visitors were encouraged to pick up a card with photo and life story of an individual whose life had been touched, for good or ill, by war and disease, with a reveal at the end of the exhibit as to whether one had lived or died. My nurse, I was happy to discover, lived.

Seeing all this, I was in rapture, well aware that there were not many men among the other visitors, and those who were there looked as if they were patiently enduring a necessary but painful medical procedure. It is probably not as true now as it was then, but in my boyhood in rural, early-1970s California, I was likely one of the few lads anywhere who saw Florence Nightingale as a hero. She'd been so since I'd first read about her, and it was because of her lamp, carried while visiting wounded soldiers in her hospital, that I asked my mother to leave my door open when she left me for the night and shut off the light. There was something soothing, for a boy who suffered frequent nightmares, about that figure walking quietly with a light through the darkness. I imagined her in the hall, looking after the nighttime world and keeping fears at bay. All these years later, I was certainly thrilled to see a copy of the lamp Nightingale had taken with her on her rounds.

But partway through my tour of the museum, something caught my eye that did not seem to belong here. Coming closer, I saw a dog, or what had been a dog, its figure sitting alert in a glass case.

His name was Jack, and he was connected to another historically important nurse. She was Englishwoman Edith Cavell, who was executed by the Germans in

1915 for sheltering Allied soldiers and spiriting them out of Belgium, often using Jack's walks as cover for her activities.

As the plaque on his display glass case states, before being rescued by Cavell, Jack was a stray, and I knew from my own rescue dog that under these conditions they can form strong attachments to one person only, bound by a powerful loyalty and even more powerful possessiveness of the person they bond themselves to. Jack was lucky. After Cavell's execution, he was rescued yet again, this time by Cavell's friend Princess Marie de Croÿ, who served in the Belgian resistance in both the First and the Second world wars. She had witnessed the dog's suffering after Cavell's death and over the course of some months she brought him back to health, and he bonded to her as he had to Cavell.

"[Marie] sometimes loaned Jack for exhibition purposes," wrote Ernest Harold Baynes, "and at a great dog show held in Lille, he proved one of the most attractive exhibits." Jack was especially meaningful to soldiers who had been nursed by Cavell, much as Rags, the Paris stray who became mascot to the American First Division in the last months of the Great War, was smuggled to the United States, and there became a symbol of hope for veterans who remembered him from battles and revered him for the lives he had saved. No doubt thanks to Cavell's former patients, and to the memorialization of her heroism, "more than a thousand photographs of the famous dog were sold for the benefit of the French Red Cross."[1]

After seven years in Princess de Croÿ's home, Jack died after a short illness. He was likely around eighteen years old. Like Station Jim, the railway collection dog of

Slough, he was given over to a taxidermist. Jack as stuffed specimen was given to the Imperial War Museum in London and, as it happened, for my visit to the Florence Nightingale Museum, he was fortuitously there on loan as part of a temporary Great War nursing exhibit.

I had come to the Florence Nightingale Museum to learn more about Florence Nightingale, and instead, I found myself on one knee before Jack, partly in the reverence I felt for this brave little dog, partly to study him more closely, as he was, frozen in time; and I thought of his legacy, wondering how he reacted and adjusted to Cavell's disappearance and the start of a new life, ending up a symbol of animal bravery and inspiration during a war no animal ever caused, in which so many animals were conscripted to serve.

Jack was also a reminder of what it must have been like, in late September 1920, to see Muggins's preserved body on display in Victoria almost a year to the day since he had had his head patted by the Prince of Wales.

At a fair on September 24 at the Willows in Oak Bay, on the stand set up for the Junior Red Cross, "the mortal remains of 'Muggins' of 'war days' fame were mounted," reported the *Daily Colonist*. "Nearly everyone passing this stand had a minute to spare for that one time heroic war worker," patting his head as so many had tried to do when he was alive, when he, too busy for sentimental human emotions, had turned away to his next task. In the October 9, 1920, issue of the *Victoria Daily Times*, Muggins is seen in a news brief with a photo showing him standing in an aquarium-like box in the Junior Red Cross Exhibit at Willows Fair.[2]

As preservation work goes, and based only on fuzzy newspaper photos, we can see that Muggins's immortal shell, like that of Jack, looked more or less like the living dog, had Muggins been pressed into a pose and then been frozen that way through some enchantment that preserved his form but robbed it of soul.

We do not know the name of the Victoria taxidermist responsible for preparing the dog's body, but we know Dr. Keown undertook to remove the pelt to begin the process, as part of the post-mortem.

What became of the body itself is anyone's guess. Only one source that I can find, that of American Samuel Brown Kirkwood, who though writing in 1922 America seems to have met Muggins in person and been acquainted with the facts of his last days, states that the dog was "buried, as the soldier he was, with full military honors." Where Muggins's body was buried is a mystery; there are no hints of such a burial in the local newspapers or any preserved memories of Victorians alive and aware of him at the time. Perhaps his remains were cremated; perhaps the Woodwards buried them in the backyard of their Gorge Road home.[3]

The Red Cross may have been behind this effort to preserve at least the outward shell of Muggins for posterity. In Muggins's *Daily Colonist* obituary, it was reported that the organization "intend having the body mounted, and it is understood they are requesting the Provincial Government to place this in the Parliament Buildings here until such time as the Victoria war memorial is established."[4]

He would have joined many other creatures on display there.

At the time of Muggins's death, the Legislature housed an ethnological museum, founded in 1886, that would form the kernel of the Royal British Columbia

Museum. Amid the ornate Victorian interior of the east wing, preserved specimens of fauna of British Columbia stood about, in and outside glass cases, with the stiff, unfocussed alertness, more like the stance of fear, of professionally stuffed animals.

Writer Stephen Hume, who visited the Legislature museum in his 1950s boyhood, recalls: "The old museum remembered from childhood flaunted all the imposing trappings that romanticized colonial hubris—Romanesque arches, Greek columns, pilasters, cornices and tiled mosaics, all the sympathetic magic of imperialism, symbols of past glory invoked to inflate one's own."[5]

Even at the time of Muggins's death, the Victorian obsession with collecting, classifying, and commemorating, was fully in force, as was, in this most British of Canadian cities, the need to do so to showcase mankind's and, by extension, Great Britain's, dominion over every living thing, as certified by conquest and the Bible. What is meant by the phrase, in Muggins's obituary, that his body would be kept at the museum until the construction of a war memorial (presumably the planned cenotaph which was unveiled in July 1925 on the Legislature grounds, near where Muggins collected for the Great War Veterans Association), is unclear. Did someone suggest that Muggins be interred near or in the cenotaph? What we know for certain, though, is that Muggins's body was not to be displayed at the Legislature. But he continued to be brought out for special occasions by the Red Cross, appearing again at the fair at the Willows standing atop the Junior Red Cross table as late as 1924.[6]

Then, for about a dozen years, Muggins disappears. When he comes back into the frame of the public eye,

Grant Hayter-Menzies

in the summer of 1936, we also see Beatrice again. For she, too, had taken leave of what had been for her the busy public stage, and the scene of Muggins's tragic end, that was Victoria.

It would be easy to assume the Woodwards left because they couldn't live with the memories indelibly soaked into every street corner, every inch of polished wood in the Empress Hotel, of Muggins. In fact, we don't know why the Woodwards left Victoria, where George Woodward had a steady job with the city, and where Beatrice had built for herself a legacy of volunteerism par excellence.

By June 1921, George and Beatrice were living in Vancouver; nine years later, they were in the United States, living in Los Angeles and operating the Crown Hill Apartments, a twenty-minute walk from MacArthur Park—then still called Westlake Park—in what was considered the closest thing to Paris's Champs Elysées Los Angeles could offer. George Woodward died in Los Angeles in 1933, and the city was still home to Beatrice when she travelled to Victoria in August 1936, carrying with her a number of photos of Muggins.

Evidently Muggins's body was still considered Beatrice's property while in the care of the Red Cross because she now gave his preserved figure to the Army and Navy Veterans in Canada, Unit 12, in Victoria. Along with the photographs, "Muggins, stuffed, and in a glass case, is [to be] mounted over the main entrance in the branch," on the inside of the building, after the fashion of nineteenth century military mascots and famed railway collection dogs in England.[7]

Yet unlike those mascots, Muggins was not to remain in situ. There is no rest for heroes. Another world war was to conscript him out of "retirement" to serve his country again in another horrific global conflict which, once again, enlisted living animals to the service of warfare.

What we could now call a thrift store—a shop selling used items, typically donated to fund a charitable cause—first had its start in Victoria in December 1915, when it was established by Mr. and Mrs. Henry Pearce to benefit the Red Cross.[8]

A few weeks after war was declared in September 1939, the Red Cross Superfluities Store made the news. "Famous Muggins Plays New War Role" stated the headline. "The dog was mounted by an expert taxidermist after his death," reports the article, "and the mounted specimen has been loaned to the Red Cross Superfluities Store at 1218 Government Street, where he stands as a symbol of devotion and loyalty to be admired by passers-by." It was noted that "the dog looks exactly as he did when alive," his collection boxes attached to his harness. The store even put out a special postcard bearing a photograph of the living Muggins, the verso giving a brief summary of the dog's life and legacy.[9]

Meanwhile, concurrent with the display of Muggins's mounted figure, efforts were reported to be underway by the Superfluities Store "to find another dog which might be trained to execute a task similar to that performed by Muggins. Who has another clever white Spitz to loan for this worthwhile cause?"[10]

In November, they received an answer, though not one that entirely fitted the request. Mrs. G.C. Bloomfield volunteered her dog, Victory, a St. Bernard pup, "who will begin next week to collect for the Red

Cross superfluities store . . . where special quarters are being prepared for him in one of the Government Street windows." Not stinting to put on the pressure, the Red Cross stated they hoped Victory might at least match the $25,000 Muggins had raised in his three years of collecting. A photo of Victory was printed with the article, showing a floppy young St. Bernard gazing up earnestly, a Red Cross banner waving behind him and a round tin marked with the red cross at his large feet.[11]

In grim consonance with the terrible war for which he was collecting donations, Victory died in 1939, the year war was declared. Mrs. Bloomfield, it was reported, had already set about obtaining another St. Bernard puppy from a breeder in New Westminster. But nothing seems to have come of the effort, as we hear no more of a collecting dog at the Superfluities Store, at least one that was still alive.[12]

And that, too, is the last we hear, in terms of newsprint, of Muggins.

The war's beginning, its fight, its victory over evils still being unpacked by historians today, the world's return to some semblance of equilibrium, all these events, along with the rising and setting sun, the passing traffic pedestrian and automobile along Government Street, the tensions of wartime and the punch-drunk thrill of peace, were reflected back for some four years from the shiny glass eyes of Muggins's silent, tensile mounted figure, steadfast in the window of the store.

People walking up and down Government Street, some pausing to look in at him, stepping inside to drop a coin in one of his collection boxes, and perhaps to pat the cold, stiff white fur; people walking up and down

Government Street who, having lost a loved one to war, could not see Muggins or anything for tears; people running and shouting up and down Government Street when victory was declared, when it seemed the world's second great nightmare of warfare was over and, it was hoped, would be the last—these too flickered in the dark glass orbs.

How many days and nights had the alert but lifeless figure stood in hot sun or through winter's chill, while coins continued to clink in the boxes he could no longer happily shake and rattle, for joy of which he could no longer register his series of sharp barks?

At some point, the expert taxidermy that had withstood the constant slow degrading of elements and caresses began to give way.

At some point—when, we do not know—the figure began to peel and crack, and the face looked more pinched, to the point where the specimen no longer resembled Muggins or even a dog, but some tattered creature that could well have been said to have been through some kind of war—the kind made not by hate but by love—and not made it to D-Day.

At some point, what was left of the figure—a long piece of skin to which white fur was still attached—was given to the family of Doris Baker, and ended up on the high shelf of a bedroom closet. When the family moved, this last piece of the corporeal Muggins disappeared and the incorporeal Muggins of memory and legend took its place.[13]

EPILOGUE

I HAVE MET ONLY A FEW AUTHENTIC CANINE mascots—dogs who are companions but something more than that.

They are attached not to one person or a few persons, but somehow, by dint of their presence in a certain environment, by something they bring to each person they meet, they become an integral part of the structure of the lives of many, a presence on whom, to borrow from Emily Dickinson, one depends for delight.

There was Alistair at Dartmouth College in New Hampshire. In 2005, I had been invited to Dartmouth to talk about a book I was working on, and spent some time in the college's history department. There I met a friendly young King Charles spaniel, whose guardian was the department secretary and who was already so beloved of the students in the department, who saw him as an indispensable therapy dog, that they put out a regular newsletter about his adventures. On that visit I was coming and going, but every time I was in the department, I was greeted by Alistair, who also comforted me in the nervous storm that always precedes a speaking engagement.

My schedule allowed me no time to pose with Alistair for a photo. I told him I'd be back soon, but that "soon" turned into nine years. By the time we were reunited on his turf, in March 2014, he had aged, had become ill, and had almost died twice, his guardian told me. "We should get that picture of you two now," she said quietly. So the morning of my departure, I trudged through snow to Carson Hall and posed with Alistair. I told him I'd see him again, but I knew I would not. Indeed, Alistair passed on a few weeks later. When I sent my condolences to Alistair's guardian, she said, "Thank you for seeing him again. He was waiting for you."

Another mascot closer to home is the famous Winston, a Labrador-golden retriever cross, whose kingdom is Muggins's old stomping grounds, Victoria's Empress Hotel.[1]

Trained to be a guide dog for the blind, Winston had proved "too friendly" for a job requiring a dog to maintain complete focus on the person they are guiding. Winston's guardian, Tracey Drake, director of public relations at the Empress, had brought Winston in with her, to find that his friendliness was not just appreciated but depended on by hotel guests. Word got around, international media came calling, and there were few pages of social or print media that did not feature Winston, showing him lying on the lobby carpet being petted or hugged or just stared at, for he's a very handsome boy.

I met Winston in person on my way through the Empress grounds one morning when he was on his way to work with Drake. Winston didn't know me from Adam, but I was greeted like an old friend, and though I'd been tensed up before our serendipitous meeting, knowing a challenging work day lay ahead of me, I was relaxed and whistling afterward, and, just as with Alistair, I felt any obstacles that seemed insurmountable were cut down to size and even made invisible, like the phantasms they were, just by having the little dog sit beside me, his great eyes gazing up at me.

And, of course, there is the handsome West Highland white terrier called MacDuff Austin-Chester, vice-regal canine consort to British Columbia's lieutenant-governor Janet Austin, who livens up many an official occasion (and shows many a human how easy it is to behave oneself in public) with his presence.

These mascots made great impressions on many others as well as on me.

And then there was the little white street dog, who seemed the very opposite—invisible, along with his homeless guardian, to everybody but me.

I never found out the dog's name. I first saw him with the man, whom I'll call Joe, on a downtown Victoria corner.

Joe was past middle age. His conversation had an articulate edge to it, but his thinking was fogged not so much by drugs—he told me he had once been a user, but had weaned himself off—as by the stunning knock on effects of unfortunate events and unfortunate choices which had brought him to this street corner in downtown Victoria, a city whose good intentions often go awry.

You can find an endless number of vastly varied scenarios among a group of people who end up on the streets—bankrupted by divorce or a failed business or poor financial choices; choosing to drop out or being kicked to the curb by addictions which local and provincial governments sometimes have a tendency to enable instead of heal, for reasons as widely diverse as the people they make an effort to serve.

All I knew of Joe was that he once told me, "I wish I knew how this had happened. It wasn't how I thought my life would be."

But he wasn't despairing—he had the little white dog, who danced around his feet and barked happily, demonstrating a dog's special blessing of living in the moment, where all humans wish they could be.

Joe said it best: "I couldn't live without him."

I could see that.

When I ran into the pair a second and third time, we began having conversations. I determined that what Joe really wanted, beyond the "spare change" he'd scrawled on a cardboard sign, was help for his dog. He told me he didn't think it was a fair deal—that his dog, who did so much for him, should have to suffer so much through him. He sketched a life on the streets that offered danger everywhere he turned. He'd been threatened by other homeless people, whose turf he had unwittingly trespassed on, and his dog had defended him against these guys with knives and with drugs in their systems, or for sale in their pockets, and nothing— as is often the case—to lose.

Concerned that if his dog was attacked he might not know where to take him for veterinary care, or afford the expense, I gave Joe the address, with map and directions, to a monthly free veterinary clinic donated by a local vet, on the premises of a downtown homeless shelter. Joe thanked me, and his dog danced around, blissfully unaware of our topic of conversation.

When I didn't see the dog with him one morning, I asked if everything was okay. Joe told me there had been another altercation with another man, whose larger dog had bitten his, "but not too badly," he said. "I took him to that vet, and now he's with a friend who has a place to live, so he can heal up." He looked at me with smiling eyes filled with tears. "Thank you for the info. I miss him so much!"

What Joe was living through is the nightmare, superadded onto the disaster, of having no place to live: the ban many shelters enforce on dogs or other animal companions of homeless people. (Out of the nine shelters listed on the City of Victoria website at the time of writing, six welcome pets all or part of the time. Joe told me he had tried them and felt as unsafe there for his dog as he did for himself; he did not elaborate details, but clearly it felt safer on the streets of down-town Victoria than in a shelter, a story replicated many times over among the city's homeless, and a large part of the irony underscoring official efforts to help people like Joe.)

An urban myth has been making the rounds of Victoria for years, according to which rough sleepers can claim more benefits, or play on more sympathy, if they have an animal with them, sitting behind the card-board sign.

This may be true to a degree, at least in terms of a cute dog's uses in attracting attention; no human being is immune to opportunism or a cynical ploy for sympa-thy, and animals are the means of making money in too many depressing ways to count. Joe seemed different. He exercised a protectiveness over the dog that he did not extend to himself. Feeling himself worthless, except insofar as he merited the love of a dog, he would have given his life to keep it safe.

Without his dog, Joe didn't know who he was. Above all, it seemed to me that without his dog, he didn't know why he was here. Where many on the streets of our city seemed to need the pharmaceutical amnesia provided by street drugs, Joe seemed to need his dog as a sturdy lifeline to the real in life. Such a little being to keep a large, grieving, and confused man connected and grounded.

There is a wide gap, I realize, between being homeless (or, in the constantly shifting newspeak coined by bureaucracy, unhoused) and being a soldier on a battlefield. I am not claiming that choices thought good at the time, or choices made in genuine despair or drug euphoria or utter carelessness, brought Joe to the streets of Victoria as the siren song of war brought my grandfather to the killing fields of the Somme and Passchendaele. But whatever our battle, and however we got there, we don't want to feel we're alone. How many soldiers, after months in the trenches of Great War France or the deserts of the eastern Mediterranean, felt themselves grounded, despite walking war's tightrope between life and death, because a dog—a mascot or a stray or a professional dispatch carrier or *chien sanitaire*—was there to see, touch, comfort with memories of childhood pets in happier times?

In this way, I saw my homeless friend and his pup as no different, because Joe was waging a battle, too, one even more terrible than in actual war because Joe's enemies were wholly invisible: they were the enemy within, and their battle plan is the antithesis of military strategy. They had stunned this man with a kind of shell shock, left him in a state of constant disbelief about what had happened to his life, and no idea what to do to survive. He needed his little white dog as antidote to the despair that overwhelms all who fight without any assurance that an armistice is just around the bend. The dog was Joe's hope that, even in the cold darkness, there was promise of light and warmth.

To those who think it sentimental, if not insane, to recognize deep awareness of expressed emotion we easily assign to human beings, or pay to see recreated by actors on stage or screen, but cannot believe are enjoyed by animals, I have only my own experiences as counter argument.

I once visited a sanctuary (SAINTS) on the British Columbia mainland, one expressly for domestic and farm animals considered too old or ill to be bothered with, too expensive to treat or cure, or impacted by a human guardian's old age or ill health,[2] I met many of these animals, almost all ill, some terminally so. Even with the care and pain medications they were given in this place, along with love many may not even have recognized, having never known it before, wary cats stared back at me; dogs glanced away or fixed me with the steady hard gaze we see in a human being who has never known a moment's affection. And I met others, responsive to the care they were receiving, and perhaps still able to hang on to an ideal of love that even abandonment and abuse could not kill. Every personality imaginable was there to greet me that day. Weariness, curiosity, distrust, affection, the gleam in a dog's eye that seems to say, "Is it you, come back to get me? Are you the one?"

I saw something else that afternoon. A large and very old, very sick dog was lying on his soft bed, and when he saw me he struggled to his feet, eyes flickering with some undying and untraceable fondness for somebody we will never know but whom he could not forget. Then his bowels gave way, and at the same time his back legs gave out, and there he lay, the sweet old man, in diarrhea that filled the room with harsh stench. Volunteers hurried to him with soothing sounds; one loved him as the other lifted him and cleaned him and took away the bedding, to be replaced with fresh blankets and pillows. I sensed he was looking at me, and he was, and it was the same look I once saw in the eyes of an elderly and infirm friend, whom I was visiting in a care facility. He had had a similar accident, and the look of fright, of disbelief, of shame, was the same, as was the flurry of professional but caring activity to rectify the situation. I reached down to touch the dog's face and said, "Don't worry, old boy," and he looked up at me again, softer, more trusting, but just as lost, wondering where he was meant to be.

Getting old is hell. Worse than that is living unloved. Visions of past punishments for something he could not help, which may have led him to be abandoned and, finally, to be rescued by the sanctuary, filled me, and I had to walk on.

Years later, long after the handsome old dog's release from suffering, I still think of him. I saw something in the eyes of Joe's little white dog, something as unforgettable as the old boy on his bed, trying to greet me. It was a concern that seemed unlinked to hope of reward, for which he expected no treat or caress—an awareness of need and keenness to do something about it, which is a simple but truthful definition of compassion as I have come to know it.

Joe didn't have to live without the care of the white dog for him, and him for the dog, for long. He eventually returned to Joe and seemed none the worse for his bad experience. As I had done per my usual schedule, I would get off my bus in chill grey dawns, Joe would wave, the dog would greet me, and I'd give Joe doggie snacks and easy-to-open-and-dispose dog food.

When it grew colder, I brought a little jacket for the dog, and was relieved it fit. Joe and I continued to chat about all kinds of things, the dog looking up at us with interest, as if what we were trying to solve was the usual messy impediment only humans could set up for themselves; a dog's world was so much simpler.

Sometimes I wouldn't see Joe or the dog for several days, and I'd carry the treats and food packets around with me on the off chance I'd see them somewhere else. When I saw them again each time, my relief was great. But then I didn't see them again. I knew which downtown doorway Joe and the dog occupied, and when I didn't spot them there for a week or so, I looked elsewhere, without success. After a while, I stopped looking. I took the stash of treats and dog food out of my satchel, and filed away the memory of this sad, smart, confused man and the little white dog he could not live without.

I eventually stopped wondering what had happened.

Then, one evening, when I was walking Freddie in my own suburban neighbourhood north of Victoria, far from the grimy streets of downtown, I saw the little white dog again.

He was with another man, and he was standing atop a brimful shopping cart as it was rattled over uneven sidewalk. The little dog was the same as before, brave, gallant, facing straight ahead, a contrast to the man pushing the cart, who was as Joe might have been after several more years on the street. When he caught me watching, he nodded in my direction, smiled and looked at the little white dog. Then they vanished around a corner. I've never seen either of them again.

I was left not so much with the sadness of not knowing what had happened to Joe, not knowing how his dog came to be with another homeless man, not knowing what would happen to the dog, though all this haunted me enough. I was left with the poignant memory of the little dog's gallantry in whatever circumstances he found himself. He was a survivor. And he helped humans survive what they could not understand or believe they could cope with without him. And he did all this, as our dog companions do, for so little in return. As dogs on battlefields had done in human wars they had not caused, but whose fighters they comforted in quiet and saved as guns blasted overhead. As Muggins had done for people who may never have known they owed their lives to a little white dog on the streets of Victoria.

Carrying this strange sadness that I could not resolve, a sadness that I had felt since holding Muggins's medals at the Saanich Archives, believing I could commune with him and his "speaking gaze" and finding only cold metal disks on which to overlay emotion, I went back to the British Columbia archives to watch newsreels, the way many of us, in the COVID-19 pandemic that overtook our lives the following year, would binge on old movies at home in the next several months.

I don't know what I was hoping for, but I told myself I was searching for another, truer glimpse of Muggins.

As mentioned earlier in this narrative, there appears to be only the footage lasting perhaps half a minute or a bit more, showing Muggins on his stand at the corner of Government and Belleville Streets as passengers just off a ship and strolling Victorians greet him and drop coins in his collection box. This was in itself a marvel. I had searched for years, with no success, for known newsreel footage of Rags, the First Division mascot, who had enjoyed a brighter fame for a longer time than Muggins and been filmed several times, according to newspaper and other accounts. But not a shred surfaced from the sea of lost media. I was grateful to see even a few moments of Muggins in action, to see his soulful eyes, high spirits, and friendliness remembered by others, so obvious even in the scratched, brief length of historic moving film.

But I wanted to see something more. I wanted to see something impossible: some indication that Muggins took this joy always in work he was conscripted to do, that he didn't sometimes sit there afraid or confused in a sea of chattering tourists—though he must have sometimes been—that he wasn't teased or threatened by strangers, as we know he was.

Like all the newsreels I'd watched of dogs trained to work at the front in the Great War, put through the paces of carrying dispatch canisters and not flinching at sudden explosions, I wanted to see what I believed was the actual truth. That these animals had been frightened. That gallantry, like bravery, like taking joy in living in the moment, had limitations.

I didn't ever find any other newsreel footage of Muggins. It may be out there—shaky, scratchy film of a small white dog licking the hand of a small, handsome, nervous, young Prince of Wales, both with futures ahead of them, near and far, that nobody seeing them that sunny September day could have guessed or wished for them.

I wanted to try, if I could, to enter into the far-off reality these films captured, to get past the silver scrim of the medium used to do so.

But then I realized something. A whole series of newsreels, pieced together on the videotape I'd checked out, consisted of Victoria men—young men, not-so-young men—marching through the streets of the city in civilian garb, or marching down to the Harbour wearing uniforms, to board a ship; and other men, changed men, in uniforms worse for wear, marching with as much relief as they had earlier marched with zeal, back up from the Harbour to the waiting arms of family and friends.

They looked much like the men I'd seen in photos of Muggins, sitting with him on the porch of Esquimalt Convalescent Hospital, or holding him, a tiny dot of white fluff among all the men in uniform, aboard a troop ship about to head out to sea.

On them had rested the fate of nations, and many never marched back to home and family. But one thing I saw in common to all.

Dogs.

Everywhere.

No matter the crowds bursting the seams of a street, or gold-braided officers enforcing discipline with their very starched, fringed and feathered presence, there were dogs.

There were large dogs and small ones.

Dogs that wore fine collars, betraying a comfortable home.

Dogs whose ribs showed, who may have had no home to go to.

Retrievers, terriers, poodles, mutts.

All were united in a shared joy, and that joy was to be with these marching men.

Sometimes I'd watch a newsreel march and not see any dogs, and think, well, there couldn't be dogs *every* time; then, in the last seconds, the camera caught them, darting out from between pinstriped male legs, from the flowing folds of female skirts, dashing in and out between the mechanical up and down of the marching soldiers' feet. And looking up, or turning to look back; barking, tongues out with the effort of keeping up; needing to join in as if it were somehow contrary to some universal law, kept devoutly in some canine rule book, that dogs and parades must occur simultaneously.

Dogs and marching men.

And many of the men, though their officers set the tone, staring straight ahead, toward the unknown horizon of their joint purpose, looked back.

Their eyes met the dogs' gaze quickly, without moving their faces. We know now, a lot more than we did then, about the science behind what a dog's gaze can do for us. A 2009 study in Japan determined that returning the gaze of one's pet dog resulted in an increase of the "bonding hormone" oxytocin, "the same mediator that underlies many significant human contacts, including the bond between mother and child," writes John Homans. "While the hormone increases trust and attachment, it apparently doesn't make people love everybody"—it reinforces the bond between the two returning one another's gaze, as we may assume it was doing for those dogs bounding alongside marching soldiers.[3]

It's like a secret society. Some soldiers, while trying to maintain decorum, couldn't help but look down with a smile, even a grin, before restoring order, nose forward, eyes stern, yet smiling still. Few were untouched by their canine companions, ready to take part in the journey, any journey, as long as they could be with the men.

When I left the archives that afternoon, I no longer envisioned Muggins's world as a place of silver sunlight, monotone blacks and greys. It was all in living colour. It is the colour of hope. Of happy memories raised to screen out unhappy uncertainties. Of love.

And I think, in seeing it thus, I understood better than I thought I ever would what made Muggins seem to give his all in service to human-created disasters which, I will always believe, humans, not animals, should have to work to clean up.

We don't live in separate worlds, Freddie and me, Winston and guests at the Empress Hotel, the little white dog and the troubled man to whose life he gave purpose, any more than Muggins did from those who cared for him and for whom he cared.

We share the same loyalty. We share the same love.

ACKNOWLEDGEMENTS

My dog Freddie seems satisfied to receive tokens of affection in form of treats and hugs and lying abed with him snoring beside me.

These don't seem enough to me.

This little dog of mine, whom I adopted in 2010 and who has been with me through thick and thin, is the source of more joy than I can express. And his courage—tested when he was in the puppy mill from which he was rescued, then thrown into the unknown setting of normal life, with so much to learn (including what toys were and how to play with them, and that the bowl of food we gave him was all for him and would never be taken away); and, in summer and autumn 2020, with cancer diagnosis, surgery, and chemotherapy over four months—is an enormous inspiration, too.

During Freddie's surgery and recovery in hospital, my partner Rudi and I hardly knew what to do with ourselves. And when he returned, delighted to be back home with us, a light that had been doused went bright again, giving me some sense of what a loss it was to so many when Muggins, the bright beacon of canine fidelity of Great War Victoria, was no longer seen waiting at the docks or scampering through the card-rooms of liners or on his table near the Empress Hotel, and worse than Freddie's absence from our home, since Freddie came back to his people and Muggins did not.

Our animal companions give us so much, unbidden, and we seem to accord them so little, and yet they ask only to be near us, to share the adventure of life together, no matter the mood of weather or of our own human complexities. If you just watch how they handle complex situations, and how in solitude they seem to know how to draw the most benefit from the richness of a given moment, you may find, as I do, that we humans have a great deal to learn from the animals who live with us in our homes or on farms or in the wild.

So I thank you, dear Freddie, for all the hours you spend beside my desk, and all the snuggles you give me just when I need them most, and for what you have taught me about how to live life to the fullest. All dogs matter, but you are our own special star.

Without the support and love of my partner, Rudi Klauser, I could not have written this book. Thank you, honey.

My thanks go to Monica Mayes of Reigning Cats and Dogs in Sidney, BC, who has lent her compassionate ear, advice, and heart to me, through several books and book ideas and Freddie's ongoing adventure with us and the world.

Had Dr. Sylvia Van Kirk not approached me to finish what she had begun, with her many years of research and deeply felt belief that Muggins's story needed to be told, I would never have had the pleasure and honour of writing this book.

Muggins's Red Cross history would never have bloomed fully for me in my research and writing had Paul Jenkins of the Canadian Red Cross-British Columbia and Yukon not shared his knowledge and enthusiasm for Muggins and the project. My heartfelt gratitude to both Sylvia and Paul.

I also thank the following:

Margaret Broad

Bruce Davies

Dr. Arthur Diggle

Peter Grant

Suzanne Hervieux (Saanich Archives)

Jean Hughes

Connie Jensen

James Kempling

Clair Kinney

Diana Kirkwood

Aris Kourkoumelis (Windsor Castle Archives)

Joseph Lenarcik (CFB Esquimalt Naval and Military Museum)

Julie Mason

Christine O'Brien

Maureen McMichael Patterson

Diana Pedersen

Vivienne Peterson (The German Spitz and Pomeranian Project)

Jan Ross

Kelly-Ann Turkington (Royal BC Museum and Archives)

Evelyn Wolfe (Saanich Archives)

Mark Zuehlke

NOTES

Notes with author names and page numbers refer to sources listed in the bibliography.

PROLOGUE

[1] *Daily Colonist*, 22 Oct 1939, cover feature

[2] Horowitz, p. 31

[3] Peterson, p. 43

CHAPTER 1

[1] Nightingale, p. 147

[2] Oliver, p. 51

CHAPTER 2

[1] *Daily Colonist*, 22 Oct 1939, Third Section Magazine Feature

[2] Vivienne Peterson, BA email to author, 4 June 2020

[3] Edwards, *Cynographia Britannica*, "Our Friend the Pomeranian," pp. 7–9

[4] Shaw, *The Illustrated Book of the Dog*, pp. 181–182

⁵ Pomeranian Project: https://www.germanspitzandpomeranian-project.org/white-poms-summary

⁶ Longford, p. 560

⁷ The photograph of Muggins on which this information was written was found in 1974 in a business located at 780 Fort Street in Victoria (it is now in the collection of the Saanich Archives). Since before the Great War, the building, which has a second storey over two storefronts, served as a rooming house, and then other purposes, as the storefronts themselves housed various businesses, among them a beauty parlour, Lloyd-El Crafts (Ceramics), Dale's Pictures and Crafts, and Victoria Personal Computer Company, the latter closest in chronology to when the picture was found. The picture, however, could have been placed in the location at any time before 1974, by anyone; it may have been left in one of the apartments upstairs, or purchased by someone at a garage sale, or given to someone associated with 780 Fort Street. An interesting side note: professional framer John Chornoby worked out of 780 Fort Street when it was owned by Lloyd-El Crafts. Only two feet, six inches tall and possibly living with phocomelia, a rare congenital disorder that causes, among other issues, malformation of limbs, Chornoby (age eighteen) was taken by his father in 1926 to join a circus in Seattle, billed as "Seal Boy." I could find no trace of a performing career for him, but he was the same age as Muggins, also born in 1913, and may well have seen or at least known about him—he was age seven the year Muggins died. Perhaps Chornoby framed the photo? This, of course, still does not answer the question: Who wrote the note on the back of the photograph about Muggins being born in the Hull residence in Calgary? Regarding where he may have been born, a *Vancouver Daily World* piece on Muggins from 1920 states that he was born in Victoria, but there is no other reference to this and the known facts tend to not support the claim. (VDW, "Muggins Dies of Pneumonia," 14 Jan 1920, p. 1.) Another curious detail about this portrait is the label. It reads MUGGINS VICTORIA B.C., in the same lettering as the stamp used on Muggins's postcards to indicate his name and where he worked and the range of funds he had thus far collected. Perhaps the portrait was given in thanks for an especially hefty donation, as the postcards were given as souvenirs for the smaller donations made aboard ships and in the streets of downtown Victoria.

Grant Hayter-Menzies

[8] For information about Hull Services, see: https://hullservices.ca

[9] For Edith Marescaux and William Roper Berry, see Ancestry.com Ahnentafel, with sources: https://www.ancestry. com/family-tree/person/tree/75896191/person/410125621147/ facts. For W.R. Hull, see Ancestry.com Ahnentafel, with sources: https://www.ancestry.com/family-tree/person/tree/75896191/ person/32339338000/facts

[10] For a photograph of the house, see: https://archives.victoria. ca/fletcher-residence-1456-beach-drive. For Ropers at this address, see: "Oak Bay Building Permits for dwellings up to 1916," https://www.oakbay.ca/sites/default/files/archives/OakBay-100yr-buildings-DATE.pdf. For information about "Mossy Rocks" on Tudor Avenue, see: "Saanich Heritage Register 2008," Donald Luxton Associates, Inc. with Jennifer Nell Barr: https://www. saanich.ca/assets/Parks~Recreation~and~Community~Services/ Documents/Planning/Heritage%20Register%20Document%20 July%2022,%202014.pdf

[11] *Daily Colonist*, "City News in Brief," 1 Aug 1914, p. 5; *Daily Colonist*, "Missed Seattle Trip," 27 Jun 1916, p. 6

[12] See Irene Murray and Tyler Trafford, co-authors, *A Magnificent Gesture: William Roper Hull 1856–1925*, p. 34. The IODE was heavily involved in many charitable endeavours, and with this came, by later estimation, a fair amount of controversy. The Order placed special weight on white imperialism, on policies exclusionary of non-white populations, and on a colonialist conservatism that was even then on point of breaking up amid the challenges of a modern age.

[13] Allen, p. 3

[14] Heritage Register James Bay: https://victoriaheritagefounda-tion.ca/HReg/JamesB/Dallas187.html

[15] *Daily Colonist*, 8 Jul 1916, p. 5

[16] Census Returns of England and Wales, 1901. Kew, Surrey, England: The National Archives, 1901, Class: RG13; Piece: 2878; Folio: 103; Page: 17

[17] Butts, p. 66

[18] Reksten, pp. 151–153

[19] *Daily Colonist*, 8 Jul 1916, p. 5

CHAPTER 3

[1] McClung, p. 26

[2] Lugrin, *Maclean's Magazine*, pp. 15, 44–45

[3] Lyrics by Ontario-born Alfred Bryan (1871–1958)

[4] McClung, p. 29

[5] Glassford, p. 92

[6] Advertisement in *Daily Colonist* 1 June 1918, p. 1. Interesting to note that tag day events were cancelled in 1920 by Victoria city council on advice from a councillor who, cogitating in what appears to be a combined fear of anti-Prohibition activity and dire public disorder related thereto, declared the fundraisers had been technically illegal during the war—and clearly too politically charged for him to have made this complaint then—and what was to stop people using this legal laissez-faire to sell whisky on Victoria's street corners? See: https://onlineacademiccommunity .uvic.ca/victoriaredcrossworldwar1/community-events/tag-days/

[7] *Daily Colonist*, 6 Aug 1916, p. 17

[8] Menzies, p. 189, p. 192

[9] Bondesen, Chapter 7, para. 5

[10] Bondesen, Chapter 7, para. 6

[11] Blog: *Atlas Obscura*, "Station Jim": https://www.atlasobscura.com/ places/station-jim

[12] Baynes, p. 19

[13] Blog: *Londonist*, "Roy, The Dog Who Refused to Leave Euston Station": https://londonist.com/london/transport/roy-the-dog-who-refused-to-quit-euston-station

[14] Samuel Brown Kirkwood, University High Yearbook 1922, p. 54. https://digitalcollections.hclib.org/digital/collection/Yearbooks/id/94805/rec/54

[15] *Daily Colonist*, 11 Oct 1916

[16] University of Victoria, A City Goes to War project: https://onlineacademiccommunity.uvic.ca/victoriaredcrossworldwar1/community-events/tag-days/

[17] About the Blue Cross: https://web.archive.org/web/20101018201037/http://www.bluecross.org.uk/1992/About-The-Blue-Cross.html. Other charities that assist in reuniting dogs and other animals bonded to soldiers serving overseas are Nowzad (https://www.nowzad.com/), Puppy Rescue Mission (https://puppyrescuemission.org/) and War Paws (https://www.warpaws.org/).

[18] *Daily Colonist*, "Belated Tributes," Vivienne Chadwick, 19 Nov 72, p. 18

[19] Cook, p. 319

[20] *Daily Colonist*, "Belated Tributes," p. 18

[21] Diana Kirkwood email to author, 31 May 2020

[22] Samuel Brown Kirkwood, University High Yearbook 1922, p. 54; email to author from Diana Kirkwood, 15 Jul 2020.

[23] Lamb, *Empress Odyssey: A History of the Canadian Pacific Service to the Orient, 1913–45*; *BC Historical Quarterly*, pp. 4–6

[24] Lamb, pp. 9–14

[25] *Daily Colonist*, 9 Nov 1916

[26] While the Great War ravaged whole populations of Europe and the eastern Mediterranean without particular attention to one group of people over another, Jews living in the borderlands

of Russia and parts of Eastern Europe were hit hard by military incursions of German forces and those of Allies fighting to sweep them back, and Belgians, whose nation had been used as a corridor to war by Germany from the start of the conflict, soon found themselves living, and dying, in a wasteland made by warfare. This had been the status quo for both Jewish commun-ities and Belgians almost since the war's first weeks in summer 1914, and relief efforts had begun to help them virtually since the start of hostilities. These were clearly issues that touched Beatrice, most likely because so many innocent children were among the casualties of the European war. Involving Muggins in raising funds for these children, whether in Italy, Belgium, or shtetls in Russia and Poland was an indication of this concern, which was shared by many women throughout the world.

CHAPTER 4

[1] *King's Own*, issue of 3 Aug 1918, quoted in Susan R. Fisher, *Boys and Girls in No Man's Land: English–Canadian Children and the First World War*, p. 31

[2] Author conversation with Cecy Margaret Baldwin, in Victoria, in 2006. Cecy Baldwin was born in London in 1913 to an accountant father who even then was ill with tuberculosis, and a musical and creative mother who, after her husband's death, brought Cecy with her to start a new life in Canada. Cecy trained as a nurse in Calgary, then was hired as governess to the children of rancher and adventure writer R.M. Patterson at his Buffalo Head Ranch, and appeared not only in the prose but in the photographs of Patterson's work. She told an amusing story of the time the visiting Raffaela, Duchess of Leinster (1902–1993), having heard that Cecy was somehow immune to the dangers of bears, was asked by the duchess to sleep in a tent outside her cabin on the ranch, which Cecy did with barely concealed hilarity. (She smiled, years later, to read in the duchess's memoirs that she had in fact had no fear of the bears said to wander the Buffalo Head Ranch.) Cecy later served as librarian for the Dominion Experimental Farm in Saanichton, north of Victoria, until she retired.

[3] Fisher, p. 35

[4] Fisher, p. 33

[5] Fisher, p. 35

[6] Christine O'Brien email to Paul Jenkins, 26 Sep 2019;
Christine O'Brien email to author, 23 Feb 2020

[7] *Daily Colonist*, "Tag Day Benefits Military Hospitals," 4 Apr 1917,
pp. 5–6

[8] *Daily Colonist*, 24 May 1917, p. 7

[9] *Daily Colonist*, "Red Cross Society is Well Represented," 13
November 1917, pp. 9–10

[10] Bess Page, *Times Colonist*, "In Memory of Muggins," D11, 9 Nov
2003; invalided soldiers selling bonds described in Reksten,
p. 153

[11] Canada's Historic Places: https://www.historicplaces.ca/en/
rep-reg/place-lieu.aspx?id=15594&pid=0

[12] *Daily Colonist*, 1 Sep 1917, p. 7

[13] *Daily Colonist*, 1 Sep 1917, p. 7

CHAPTER 5

[1] Canada's Historic Places: https://www.historicplaces.ca/en/
rep-reg/place-lieu.aspx?id=15593&pid=0

[2] Young and McKinnon, pp. 16–19

[3] Young & McKinnon, p. 115

[4] Young & McKinnon, p. 124

[5] *Daily Colonist*, 4 Apr 1917, p. 5

[6] *Daily Colonist*, 30 Oct 1917, p. 11

[7] *Daily Colonist*, 7 Jan 1919, p. 9

[8] *Daily Colonist*, 30 Oct 1917, p. 11

[9] *Daily Colonist*, "Victoria Gives $2270 For Halifax Relief," 20 Dec 1917, p. 9

[10] *Daily Colonist*, 9 Aug 1917, p. 7

[11] *Oregon Sunday Journal*, 23 Sep 1917, p. 7

[12] *New York Times*, 6 Jan 1918, p. 5

[13] *Our Dumb Animals*, October 1917, Vol. 50, No. 5, p. 68

[14] *Our Dumb Animals*, July 1919, Vol. 52, No. 2, p. 28

[15] Clair Kinney email to author 4 May 2020; *Daily Colonist*, "Death of Horse," 9 Oct 1897

[16] *Daily Colonist*, "Dog Makes Visits to Hospital For Ear," 13 Apr 1924, p. 35

[17] *Our Dumb Animals*, July 1919, Vol. 52, No. 2, p. 28

CHAPTER 6

[1] *Spokesman-Review*, Spokane, WA, 25 Nov 1917, p. 59

[2] *Daily Colonist*, 22 Oct 1939, Third Section Magazine Feature

[3] *Vancouver Sun*, 21 Feb 1918, p. 12; *Vancouver Daily News*, 5 Aug 1918, p. 7

[4] *Victoria Daily Times*, 18 Feb 1918, p. 5

[5] *Daily Colonist*, 22 Oct 1939, Third Section Magazine Feature

[6] Samuel Brown Kirkwood, University High Yearbook 1922, p. 54. Regarding the bar pin: I examined the pin in person at the Saanich Archives on 26 October 2020.

[7] Samuel Brown Kirkwood, University High Yearbook 1922, p. 54.

[8] Diggle attestation form 5 April 1915: Canadian Over-Seas Expeditionary Force, No. 58308

⁹ Crozier attestation form 30 Nov 1915: Canadian Over-Seas Expeditionary Force, No. 213045

¹⁰ *Daily Colonist*, 24 Aug 1919, p. 22

¹¹ *Daily Colonist*, "Pup Called Vimy Ridge," 23 Feb 1918, p. 6

¹² Samuel Brown Kirkwood, University High Yearbook 1922, p. 54.

¹³ *Daily Colonist*, 13 Jun 1917, p. 8

¹⁴ *Daily Colonist*, "Pup Called Vimy Ridge," 23 Feb 1918, p. 6. A short video about Resthaven Hospital, the former sanatorium reconfigured for wounded veterans, located near Sidney (twenty-four kilometres north of Victoria), includes two photos of a white Spitz, without collar or harness, and smaller than Muggins, with convalescent soldiers and nurses at Resthaven. One of these nurses, Pearl Ross, was active at Resthaven until 1918, when she transferred to Esquimalt Military Hospital. Given the fact that it was in that year that young Vimy began to be taken the rounds to collect donations himself, it is at least possible that Pearl or another nurse from Esquimalt, with which Muggins was closely associated, brought the pup out to cheer the patients at Resthaven. If so, the dog in these photos may be the only image we have of Muggins's son. I'm grateful to Paul Jenkins for alerting me to this information. Link: https://youtu.be/mcTd3GM2DgY, produced by The Francophone Assembly of Retirees and Seniors of British Columbia https://www.afracb.ca/

¹⁵ *Daily Colonist*, 21 Jun 1918, p. 15

¹⁶ *Daily Colonist*, 26 Jan 1919, p. 7

¹⁷ *Daily Colonist*, 17 Jul 17, p. 8

¹⁸ *Daily Colonist*, 30 Aug 19, p. 15. A search of local newspaper want ads in both Victoria and Vancouver for this period reveals a saddening number of notices offering rewards for finding lost or stolen dogs, many of them valuable purebreds like Muggins (and many of them, like him, pure white).

¹⁹ *Daily Colonist*, 1 May 1919, p. 7

Muggins   177

[20] *Daily Colonist*, 1 May 1919, p. 7

[21] *Daily Colonist*, 9 Sep 1947 p. 11

[22] *Daily Colonist*, 1 May 1919, p. 7

[23] *Daily Colonist*, 4 May 1919, p. 14. The *Victoria Daily Times*, 13 Mar 1920, p. 9 ("The trouble started when Mr. Pitman arrested the late Muggins . . . ") features an article describing how the pound keeper, J. Pitman, was dismissed after continued friction between himself and members of council.

[24] *Daily Colonist*, 12 Nov 1918 p. 1

[25] *Daily Colonist*, 12 Nov 1918 p. 5

[26] *Daily Colonist*, 12 Nov 1918 p. 5

[27] *Daily Colonist*, 12 Nov 1918 p. 5

CHAPTER 7

[1] *Daily Colonist*, 28 Feb 1919, p. 7

[2] *Daily Colonist*, 28 Feb 1919, p. 7

[3] *Daily Colonist*, 7 May 1916, p. 4

[4] *Daily Colonist*, 5 Nov 1918, p. 8

[5] *Daily Colonist*, 8 Mar 1919, p. 6

[6] *Daily Colonist*, "Questions Asked Development Association Secretary Were Unique," 7 Jan 1919, p. 9

[7] *Cowichan Leader*, "Great War Veterans' Assn.," 21 Feb 1918, p. 1

[8] *Cowichan Leader*, "Great War Veterans' Assn.," 21 Feb 1918, p. 1

[9] *Daily Colonist*, 20 Aug 1919, p. 2

[10] *Daily Colonist*, 12 Jul 1919, p. 5

[11] *Daily Colonist*, 17 Jul 1919, p 11. *Daily Colonist*, 5 Sep 1919, p. 6 mentions the make of the piano, which cost $550—around $7500 Canadian today.

[12] *Daily Colonist*, 20 Jul 1919, p. 1

[13] *Daily Colonist*, 20 Jul 1919, p. 5

[14] *Daily Colonist*, 20 Jul 1919, p. 5

[15] *Daily Colonist*, "Many at Cabaret at Empress Last Night," 6 Nov 1919, p. 16. The song "Come on Papa," by Harry Ruby and Edgar Leslie, was released in 1918.

[16] "From the Archives: Kathleen Euphemia Dunsmuir," Royal Roads University, August 2014: https://crossroads.royalroads. ca/news/archives-kathleen-euphemia-dunsmuir. Kathleen Humphreys' interest in performance would include, in her forties, a gallant but unforthcoming attempt to break into Hollywood films. An inveterate volunteer in charities, she was in London, England helping out with the war effort during the Second World War when she was killed in an air raid in 1941. Interesting to note that after Muggins's death, the house where he had lived with the Ropers, 1456 Beach Drive, would be home to the Humphreys, their two children, a nursemaid, housemaid and cook (*Sixth Census of Canada*, 1921, Nanaimo 19, No. 48).

[17] *Daily Colonist*, "Many at Cabaret at Empress Last Night," 6 Nov 1919, p. 16. I was unable to locate a song that fit the article's description of "the Bamboo song" other than "Princess Pat," which dates from 1917 and would have been well known to most people in the Empress Hotel ballroom that evening.

[18] *Daily Colonist*, "Many at Cabaret at Empress Last Night," 6 Nov 1919, p. 16

[19] *Daily Colonist*, 20 Dec 1919, p. 6

[20] Related to author in Portland, Oregon in July 1998 by a great-granddaughter of the housemaid in question.

[21] Ziegler, p. 118

[22] Berton, p. 240

[23] Warwick, p. 86

[24] *A King's Story*, p. 144

[25] *A King's Story*, p.145

[26] *A King's Story*, 143–144

[27] The *Province*, Vancouver, "People Honor Prince at Victoria," 25 Sep 1919, p. 3

[28] *Winnipeg Tribune*, "Victoria Sets Pace for Vancouver Isle," 26 Feb 1936, p. 2

[29] *Winnipeg Tribune*, "Victoria Sets Pace for Vancouver Isle," 26 Feb 1936, p. 2

[30] *Daily Colonist*, 22 Oct 1939, cover

[31] Aris Kourkoumelis, Assistant Curator of Photographs at the Royal Collection Trust, Windsor Castle, searched extensively for the photograph among royal records, to no avail. Email to author, 11 April 2019. I also queried the Al Fayed Foundation (Mohammed Al Fayed, father of Dodi Al Fayed who died with Diana, Princess of Wales in Paris in 1997, purchased the Windsors' villa with contents) and Christie's, the auction house which supervised the sale of contents from the Windsor villa. Nothing was found.

CHAPTER 8

[1] *Daily Colonist*, 20 Dec 1919, p. 6

[2] *Daily Colonist*, "Chapter Receives $860 for Milk Fund," 21 Dec 1919, p. 7

[3] *Daily Colonist*, "Many at Cabaret at Empress Last Night," 6 Nov 1919, p. 16

[4] *Daily Colonist*, "Muggins Helps Santa," 24 Dec 1919, p. 6

[5] *Daily Colonist*, "Hospital Patients Have Wonderful Time," 24 Dec 1919, p. 14

[6] St. Luke's Anglican Church, Statement of Significance, 1 Apr 2004: https://www.reddeer.ca/media/reddeerca/about-red-deer/history/heritage/heritage-sites/downtown/St.-Luke's-Anglican-Church---Statement-of-Significance---1-Apr-2004.pdf

[7] University of Alberta Libraries, *Blackfoot Prayer Book*: http://peel.library.ualberta.ca/bibliography/2456.html

[8] *Daily Colonist*, "Hospital Patients Have Wonderful Time," 24 Dec 1919, p. 14

[9] *Edmonton Journal*, "The Passing of a Little Hero," N. deBertrand for the *Canadian Courier*, 23 Feb 1920, p. 4

[10] WHO, "Q&A on coronaviruses (COVID-19)." For news reports on a UK cat and a Canadian dog who became infected with COVID-19, see: "Cat diagnosed with coronavirus in first UK case of animal infection," Matthew Weaver and Jessica Elgot, the *Guardian*, 27 July 2020 (https://www.theguardian.com/world/2020/jul/27/pet-cat-diagnosed-with-covid-19-uk-government-confirms) and "A Niagara-area dog first in Canada to test positive for COVID-19," Sara Mojtehedzadeh, the *Toronto Star*, 26 October 2020: https://www.thestar.com/news/gta/2020/10/25/a-niagara-area-dog-first-in-canada-to-test-positive-for-covid-19.html 17 April 2020 | Q&A: https://www.who.int/emergencies/diseases/novel-coronavirus-2019/question-and-answers-hub/q-a-detail/q-a-coronaviruses

[11] *Daily Colonist*, "Muggins' Career Ended By Pneumonia," 15 Jan 1920, p. 7

[12] *Daily Colonist*, "Muggins' Career Ended By Pneumonia," 15 Jan 1920, p. 7

[13] Beers, *For the Prevention of Cruelty: The History and Legacy of Animal Rights Activism in the United States*, p. 75

[14] *Daily Colonist*, "Muggins' Career Ended By Pneumonia," 15 Jan 1920, p. 7

[15] *Daily Colonist*, "Muggins' Career Ended By Pneumonia," 15 Jan 1920, p. 7

[16] *Daily Colonist*, "Died of Pneumonia," 16 Jan 1920, p. 6

[17] *Daily Colonist*, "Muggins: A Tribute," 15 Jan 1920, p. 4

[18] *Daily Colonist*, "Muggins," 25 Jan 1920, p. 17

CHAPTER 9

[1] Baynes, pp. 19–20

[2] *Daily Colonist*, "Home Products Attracted Crowds," 25 Sep 1920, p. 7; *Victoria Daily Times*, "Junior Red Cross Exhibit at Willows Fair," 9 Oct 1920 (clipping in Muggins collection at Saanich Archives; no page number included).

[3] Samuel Brown Kirkwood, University High Yearbook 1922, p. 54

[4] *Daily Colonist*, "Muggins' Career Ended by Pneumonia," 15 Jan 1920, p. 7

[5] Stephen Hume, review of *The Collectors* by Patricia Roy, *Focus Magazine*, 4 Jan 2019: https://www.focusonvictoria.ca/janfeb2019/patricia-roys-the-collectors-r4/

[6] *Daily Colonist*, "Junior Red Cross," 21 Aug 1924, p. 7

[7] *Daily Colonist*, "Present 'War Dog' to Club," 2 Aug 1936, p. 5

[8] *Daily Colonist*, "Superfluities Great Aid to Red Cross," 5 Aug 1917, p. 17

[9] *Daily Colonist*, "Famous Muggins Plays New War Role," 24 September 1939, p. 2

[10] *Daily Colonist*, "Successor for Muggins," 26 Sep 1939, p. 4

[11] *Daily Colonist*, "St. Bernard Will Collect for Red Cross," 16 Nov 1939, p. 5

[12] The *Province*, "Muggins of the Red Cross," P.W. Luce, 14 Mar 1940, p. 4

[13] Another Canadian dog involved with the Great War whose afterlife touches on Muggins's is Sable Chief, the Newfoundland dog who was mascot of the Royal Newfoundland Regiment from 1914 to 1919. Like Muggins, Sable Chief wore a collection

box for donations to the British Red Cross Prisoners of War fund, and in 1917 travelled to Scotland with the Regimental Band; he was photographed in front of Buckingham Palace and attended other special events where a number of dignitaries met him. Like Muggins, Sable Chief lived a short life: he was accidentally killed by a truck in 1919. His body was preserved by a taxidermist and later shipped back to Newfoundland, where, like Muggins's, it was exposed to gradually destructive natural elements and the caresses of those who remembered and honoured him. By 2006, Sable Chief's pelt was falling apart. A fundraising drive was mounted to restore him, and thus repaired, he is on display at the Provincial Museum of Newfoundland and Labrador in St. John's. See https://en.wikipedia.org/wiki/Sable_Chief and https://www.therooms.ca/exhibits/now/beaumont-hamel-and-the-trail-of-the-caribou

EPILOGUE

[1] CBC News, "Would-be guide dog triumphs as greeter at Victoria's Empress Hotel," 11 Jan 2019: https://www.cbc.ca/news/canada/british-columbia/would-be-guide-dog-triumphs-as-greeter-at-victoria-s-empress-hotel-1.4975838

[2] SAINTS is acronym for Senior Animals in Need Today Society. It is located in Mission, British Columbia, a little over an hour's drive southeast of Vancouver. Founded by Carol Hine in 2004, SAINTS is a refuge for animals, often elderly and ill and discarded because of illness and age or human circumstances, who but for this sanctuary would otherwise have no place to go. Many are adopted into loving families; others live their last days at SAINTS in loving care with expert medical attention to their needs. To find out more, check out their website: https://www.saintsrescue.ca/

[3] Homans, p. 27

SOURCES

PERIODICALS, VIA ONLINE ARCHIVES

Canadian Courier

Cowichan Leader

Daily Colonist (former iteration of the *Times Colonist*, Victoria, BC)

Edmonton Journal

Focus Magazine (Victoria, BC)

The New York Times

Oregon Sunday Journal (Portland, OR)

Our Dumb Animals

Spokesman–Review (Spokane, WA)

The Province

Toronto Star

Vancouver Sun

Winnipeg Tribune

BIBLIOGRAPHY

Allen, Ralph. *Ordeal By Fire*. New York: Doubleday & Co., 1961.

Baynes, Ernest Harold. *Animal Heroes of the Great War*. New York: MacMillan, 1925.

Beers, Diane L. *For the Prevention of Cruelty: The History and Legacy of Animal Rights Activism in the United States*. Athens, OH: Ohio University Press, 2006.

———. *For the Prevention of Cruelty: The History and Legacy of Animal Rights Activism in the United States,* Athens, OH: Ohio University Press, 2006.

Bekoff, Marc and Jessica Pierce. *The Animals' Agenda: Freedom, Compassion, and Coexistence in the Human Age*. Boston: Beacon Press, 2017.

Bekoff, Marc. *The Emotional Lives of Animals*. Novato, CA: New World Library, 2007.

Berton, Pierre. *Marching to War: Canada's Turbulent Years 1899–1953,* Toronto: Doubleday Canada, 2001.

Bindon, Kathryn M. *More Than Patriotism*. Toronto: Personal Library, 1979.

Bondesen, Jan. *Amazing Dogs: A Cabinet of Canine Curiosities*. Stroud, Gloucestershire: Amberley Publishing, 2012 (ebook).

Butts, Edward. *Wartime: The First World War in a Canadian Town*. Toronto: James Lorimer & Company Ltd., Publishers (ebook).

Carmichael, Jacqueline Larson. *Heard Amid the Guns: True Stories from the Western Front, 1914–1918*. Victoria: Heritage House Publishing Company, Ltd., 2020.

Cook, Tim. *The Secret History of Soldiers: How Canadian Survived the Great War,* Toronto: Penguin Canada, 2018.

———. *Vimy: The Battle and the Legend*. Toronto: Penguin Canada, 2017.

Cooper, Jilly. *Animals in War*. London: Corgi Books, 2000.

Coren, Stanley. *The Pawprints of History: Dogs and the Course of Human Events*. New York: The Free Press/Simon & Schuster, 2002.

Cuthbertson, Ken. *The Halifax Explosion: Canada's Worst Disaster*. Toronto: HarperCollins, 2017.

Edward, Duke of Windsor. *A King's Story: The Memoirs of the Duke of Windsor*. New York: Thomas Allen Ltd., Canada, 1951.

Edwards, Sydenham. *Cynographia Britannica*, no page numbers; listed under chapter "Canis Pomeranus, Pomeranian, or Fox Dog," London: C. Whittingham, 1800.

Fisher, Susan R. *Boys and Girls in No Man's Land: English–Canadian Children and the First World War*, New York: University of Toronto Press, 2011.

Gammel, Irene. *I Can Only Paint: The Story of Battlefield Artist Mary Riter Hamilton*. Montreal: McGill-Queen's University Press, 2020.

Glassford, Sarah. *Mobilizing Mercy: A History of the Canadian Red Cross*, Montreal: MQUP, 2017.

Gordon, Sophie. *Noble Hounds and Dear Companions: The Royal Photograph Collection*. London: Royal Collection Enterprises Ltd., 2007.

Hayter-Menzies, Grant. *From Stray Dog to World War I Hero: The Paris Terrier Who Joined the First Division*. Lincoln, NE: Potomac Books/University of Nebraska Press, 2015.

Homans, John. *What's A Dog For? The Surprising History, Science, Philosophy, and Politics of Man's Best Friend*, New York: Penguin Books, 2012.

Horowitz, Alexandra. *Inside of a Dog: What Dogs See, Smell, and Know*. New York: Scribner, 2009.

Ilyin, Olga. *White Road: A Russian Odyssey, 1919–1923*, New York: Holt, Rinehart and Winston, 1984.

Johns, Rowland, editor. *Our Friend the Pomeranian*. New York: E.P. Dutton & Co., 1936.

Lamb, W. Kaye. *Empress Odyssey: A History of the Canadian Pacific Service to the Orient, 1913–45*, BC Historical Quarterly, Vol. XII, Victoria, BC, January 1948, No. 1.

Lemish, Michael G. *War Dogs: A History of Loyalty and Heroism.* Washington, DC: Potomac Books, 2008.

———. *War Dogs: A History of Loyalty and Heroism.* Washington, DC: Potomac Books, Inc., 2008.

Longford, Elizabeth. *Queen Victoria: Born to Succeed*, New York: Harper & Row, 1964.

MacDonogh, Katharine. *Reigning Cats and Dogs: A History of Pets at Court Since the Renaissance.* New York: St. Martin's Press, 1999.

MacMillan, Margaret. *The Road to 1914: The War That Ended Peace.* New York: Random House, 2014.

Masson, Jeffrey. *Dogs Never Lie About Love: Reflections on the Emotional Lives of Dogs.* New York: Vintage, 1998.

McClung, Nellie. *The Next of Kin: Those Who Wait and Wonder*, Toronto / Boston: Thomas Allen / Houghton Mifflin, 1917.

Menzies, Lucy. *The First Friend*, London: George Allen & Unwin Ltd., 1922.

Morton, Desmond. *A Military History of Canada.* Edmonton: Hurtig Publishers, 1985.

———. *A Short History of Canada.* Toronto: McClelland & Stewart, third rev. ed., 1997.

Murray, Irene and Tyler Trafford. *A Magnificent Gesture: William Roper Hull 1856–1925.* Calgary: Hull Services, 2012.

Nicolson, Juliet. *The Great Silence: Britain from the Shadow of the First World War to the Dawn of the Jazz Age.* New York: Grove/Atlantic, 2009.

Nightingale, Florence. *Notes on Nursing: What It Is and What It Is Not.* London: Harrison, 1860

Oliver, Mary. *Dog Songs.* New York: Penguin, 2013.

Peterson, Dale. *The Moral Lives of Animals*. New York: Bloomsbury Press, 2012.

Reksten, Terri. *More English Than the English: A Very Social History of Victoria*. Victoria: Orca Books, 1991.

Segger, Martin and Douglas Franklin. *Victoria: A History in Architecture 1843–1929*. Watkins Glen, NY: The American Life Foundation and Study Institute, 1970.

Shaw, Vero. *The Illustrated Book of the Dog*, London: Cassell, Petter, Galpin & Co., 1881.

Shipman, Pat. *The Animal Connection: A New Perspective on What Makes Us Human*. New York: W.W. Norton, 2011.

Shipman, Pat. *The Animal Connection: A New Perspective on What Makes Us Human*. New York: W.W. Norton, 2011.

Tooley, Sarah. *The Life of Florence Nightingale*. London: Cassell and Company, Ltd., 1914.

Warwick, Christopher. *King George VI and Queen Elizabeth: A Portrait*. London: Sidgwick & Jackson, 1985.

Woollcott, Alexander. *Verdun Belle and some others*. New York: Grosset & Dunlap, 1928.

Young, Kathryn A. and Sarah M. McKinnon. *No Man's Land: The Life and Art of Mary Riter Hamilton*, Winnipeg: University of Manitoba Press, 2017.

Ziegler, Philip. *King Edward VIII: The Official Biography*, Toronto: HarperCollins Canada Ltd., 1990.

INDEX

1st Infantry Division (US), 13, 15, 18, 20, 143
19th Battalion, 98
20th Battalion, 98
102nd Infantry Regiment (US), 19

Aged Ladies' Home, 89
Alexandrovna, Grand Duchess Olga, 26
Alistair (dog), 151–52
Allen, Ralph, 34
Amputation Club of Victoria, 85
animals, 7–10, 11, 17, 18, 58, 92, 157
  See also dogs; horses
animal sanctuaries, 157–58
Army and Navy Veterans in Canada, 147
Army Medical Corps, 37
Austin, Janet, 153

Baines, Herbert, 74
Baines, Kathleen, 74
Baker, Doris, 4–5, 123, 130, 131, 150
Baldwin, Cecy, 71–72
Balkan Wars, 58
Banister, Emmeline, 29
Bantam regiment, 75
Barnard, Francis Stillman, 5, 40, 111, 123, 131
Baynes, Ernest Harold, 18, 55, 143Bay Street Armoury, 51, 121
Beacon Hill Park, 110–11, 123
Belgian Relief Fund, 47
Benedict, A.L., 91
Black Watch, 108
Bloomfield, Mrs. G.C., 148, 149
Blue Cross, 57, 58, 111
Boer War, 33, 119
Bondesen, Jan, 54–55
Breakwater District, 35

Grant Hayter-Menzies

Grant Hayter-Menzies

Grant Hayter-Menzies is a biographer and historian specializing in the lives of extraordinary and unsung heroes of the past, notably the role of animals in times of war. He is also literary executor of playwright William Luce. He lives in Sidney, British Columbia, with his dog, Freddie, and partner, Rudi. For more information, visit grantmenzies.wixsite.com/author.

Photo by Rudi Klauser